TWELVE STONES
Crossing into the Promise Land

By

Kay P. Adkins

xulon
PRESS

Table of Contents

A Special Thank You

There are so many people without whom this book could not have been written. First there is my husband who is my most avid supporter and encourager. He was the one who would cheer me on when I wanted to quit. He was the one who doggedly read through a mountain of pages to help me decide what should and shouldn't be included. He was the one who would read and say, "I don't understand," and I would know something had to be changed.

And there are my children, my biggest fan club, who, miracle of miracles, think I can do no wrong. They are all special to me and I love each of them dearly.

There is little mentioned in the book about our son, but that is only because he, thankfully, had his life pretty well straightened out at the time it was written and he didn't require a lot of my time and effort. But just because he isn't mentioned often doesn't mean he hasn't been an inspiration to me. He was our first born, our only son, our starter child, and there were times he paid dearly for that "privilege," but he never complained and actually feels he had a good child-hood (more proof to me of the grace of God).

Our oldest daughter, in comparison, is mentioned often in the book. God has used her to teach me more than I have learned from any other person. I love her dearly and look hopefully to God for the day when she will be free from the demons that have so haunted her life.

And then our youngest daughter, the sunshine of our lives. She has cheered me on through every step of this book and her encouragement, love, suggestions, and unconditional support have been invaluable to me. And she is also the one who has given me a second chance to be the grandmother that I was "too busy" to be when the others were born and growing up.

The fact that you can even read this is because of Desiree Simmons who did the editing for me. She painstakingly worked her way through all my strange words and thoughts and dozens of hyphens, putting words in the right order and punctuation marks in the right places. I owe you big, Desiree.

Most of all, I want to thank my God, who "*...brought me up also out of an horrible pit, out of the miry clay, and set my feet upon a rock, and established my goings,*" (Psalm 40:2). It is only because of Him that I can even put two words together. It was He who taught me that I truly can do nothing without Him (John 15:5), but that with Him, all things are possible (Mark 10:27). I anxiously await the day that I see Him face to face.

Stone #1

Life in the Pit

He brought me up also out of an horrible pit, out of the miry clay, and set my feet upon a rock, and established my goings.
Psalm 40:2

He brought me up also out of an horrible pit, out
of the miry clay, and set my feet upon a rock, and
established my goings.
Psalm 40:2

This verse is a perfect description of the miracle God
performed for me. My entire life, until the age of 45,
was lived in the pit of destruction, or what I frequently refer
to as the pits of hell.

My childhood was spent in an extremely dysfunctional
environment full of alcoholism and abuse. And while that
may be a reason for sliding into the pit, it is not an excuse.
Many people come from a much worse background than I
did and don't turn their lives over to the pit keeper. No, the
pit I wallowed in was one of self-destruction. I have no one
to blame but myself.

Whether we admit it or not, we all have a bit of voyeur
in us. We like to see bits and pieces of other people's lives,
especially the unsavory parts. There are not enough pages
within any book to hold all that's unsavory from my past, but
I occasionally give you a glimpse into it in the pages of this
book so that you will understand where I'm coming from.

There was not a whole lot known about alcoholism when
I was young. For instance, it wasn't known that the tendency
is hereditary. I like to think I would have made some different
choices had I known, but in my heart I know the knowledge
would not have changed anything.

I took my first drink when I was 14-years-old. That drink
was the initial step in a 32 year journey to the bottom of the
pit. Looking back, I'm amazed at the incredible punishment
the body and the mind can take without breaking. During
that 32 years, I married, had three children, raised them
(albeit with many problems of their own), held down good
jobs with ever increasing levels of responsibility, and kept

a marriage together against incredible odds. But don't pat me on the back. Anything good that may have been accomplished was straight from God. Why He carried me all that time when I was so totally oblivious to everything but myself is beyond my comprehension.

Finally one night I hit the bottom of the pit with such a thud I was sure it must have been heard around the world. I felt I wanted to die but I was afraid to. My only other option was to quit drinking, but I was equally afraid of that. I didn't know how to live without drinking. However, God didn't bring me through the previous 45 years just so I could end it all. He showed me how to live without the alcohol one day at a time and, occasionally, one hour at a time. I know there are some who say an alcoholic is never recovered but always recovering, but my God heals completely. When He pulled me from the pit, He set my feet upon a Rock—there will never be "that next drink" for me.

They soon forgat his works; they waited not for his counsel: but lusted exceedingly in the wilderness, and tempted God in the desert. And he gave them their request...
Psalm 106:13-15

Like the Israelites who wandered the wilderness for 40 years, I pretty much want what I want when I want it. And like them, God has, on occasion, allowed me to wander around and around and around the same mountain in order to learn that I don't always know what's best for me. And sometimes, His most effective way of teaching this lesson is to give me exactly what I think I want.

When I was raising my family, working, trying to keep my heart from completely breaking over an often absent and errant husband, and all the while drinking more and more, I always thought I knew what would make everything better. My solutions would change frequently as I tried one thing after another, always ending in failure.

I thought my mother was bound to admire me, love me, and be proud of me if I could just discover what it was she was looking for in a daughter. I was certain my husband would stay home and love me if I could just be sweeter, be prettier, cook better, keep a cleaner house, make more money on my job, do more for him, etc. I knew my children would be better behaved if I could just find the right combination between mother and friend.

Surely my employers would think highly of me if I could put in enough overtime and do enough extra work. And those I was in charge of would consider me wonderful if I helped them out enough with their work and overlooked their infractions and occasionally allowed them to come in late and leave early. Friends? They would have to love me and stay with me if I agreed with everything they said or did and never asked for their help, but always be ready to help them out with whatever their current need.

God would let me do all these things my own way, but like the Israelites, I didn't learn very fast. Instead of realizing I needed to be doing things God's way, I was certain the problem was in my methods. And so would begin the search for a new method.

As I neared the end of my journey through alcoholism, our youngest child was preparing to leave for college. I had thought for several years that this would be the perfect situation because I could drink as much as I wanted without having to worry about the disapproval of anyone. So God "gave me my request." Within nine months of this "freedom", I was in a treatment center wanting to die. Slowly God began to show me that following His ways is *always* best, regardless of any ideas I may have to the contrary. My prayer today is that God will keep me in His perfect will and His perfect timing and to slap me up beside the head if I begin thinking I know better than He does. I don't ever want Him to give me my requests when they are not *His* desire for me. Been there and done that.

...but this one thing I do, forgetting those things which are behind, and reaching forth unto those things which are before.
Philippians 3:13

When I entered recovery from alcoholism, it was necessary for me to look to my past. I needed to get as much of a hold as possible on my reasons for drinking. Looking at the past helped me to recognize pitfalls and know the dangers I needed to avoid. Once I had analyzed the reasons for my alcoholism, accepted responsibility for my past, and asked God's forgiveness for the many sins I had committed, it was time to move on.

Paul had a past which held no pride for him, having been instrumental in the persecution of many Christians. He had been very legalistic and "religious," one of the very types Jesus scorned. Yet, Paul knew an absolute truth, one that all of us with a "past" need to learn: it was what it was, and we can't change it. We must deal with our past and then put it behind us and move forward to those things which are ahead.

As an alcoholic who was serious about recovery (it was literally a "do or die" situation for me), I spent a good portion of my first sober year in various 12-step support group meetings. They are a Godsend, helping to smooth the road for the newly recovering. But after a while I began to notice a strange phenomenon. There were people who had been in these groups and attending the meetings for years. I'm not talking about those who feel called to remain to help the newcomers. That is a special ministry and God blesses those who answer that call. No, I'm speaking of those who seem to have traded their addiction for a dependence on the group. These people are stuck, unable (or unwilling) to move forward and become recovered instead of always recovering. They want to constantly talk about their past, their childhood, the people who have hurt them, the people who are still hurting them, etc.

I know the popular belief is that alcoholics, addicts, etc. are never recovered but are only one step, drink, fix, whatever, from full-blown practicing addiction. In one sense, I agree. If I were to ever take another drink, I could easily slip back into that hell. But I believe I am recovered in that God has completely removed the desire to drink from me. My Bible says He has healed me, not He is healing me. But it is our responsibility to receive that healing, and we do that by forgetting what lies behind and reaching forward to what lies ahead.

...our inequities are increased over our head, and our
trespass is grown up unto the heavens.
Ezra 9:6

I have been sick for about the last ten days, ten guilt ridden days. I haven't felt like doing anything so have pretty much stayed on the couch sleeping and watching movies. Any doctor will tell you that the best thing for a cold is lots of liquids and lots of rest. So why would following doctor's orders produce such guilt within me? I wish I knew the answer to that.

As I pondered this craziness, I realized I have spent most of my life feeling guilty. I will be the first to admit that most of it was earned, but not so the last few years. Yet guilt still pervades my very being.

I've read that at some point in a sexually abused child's life, he passes the point of feeling ashamed of what's happening to him and becomes ashamed of himself. I was sexually abused for much of my childhood and perhaps this is where the guilt started for me. But, though it may have begun there, it has spilled over into every aspect of my life.

I remember, even as a young person, always feeling guilty. I could never seem to please my mother, no matter what I did. Of course, I felt it was because there was something wrong with me, as kids always do in that situation. Even knowing now that the problem was not with me doesn't change that childhood feeling of inadequacy.

In my early teen years, I discovered that alcohol took the edge off the guilt—at least while I was drinking. Inevitably, however, the sober moments were laden not only with the regular guilt, but the added guilt brought on by the drinking and the lifestyle that accompanied it: skipping school, unfavorable companions, shoplifting, etc.

As a young adult I married and had a family, but the drinking continued. To my already guilt-ridden soul, I added the certain knowledge that my husband's lack of commitment to our marriage was my own fault. As the children grew into teenagers, I also took upon myself the blame for all their problems (and rightfully so in many of the situations).

But that is all in the past. I've grown close to God and have acknowledged and accepted His forgiveness for all those past sins. Though there are many things from those years I regret, I don't dwell on them and wallow in guilt over them.

No, my problem now is the hundreds of small things that currently keep me in a constant state of guilt. What is the answer? I know, as with everything, the answer is God. I just don't know for sure, yet, how to approach the situation. But I'm confident God will lead me to the answer.

*...that thou mayest keep the law of the Lord thy God.,
then shalt thou prosper...*
1 Chronicles 22:12-13

When creating the world, God made certain rules, or material laws. Rules like whatever a man sows, this he will also reap (Galatians 6:7). Or, whoever believes in Jesus will have eternal life (John 3:16). Or, if you do well, your countenance will be lifted up (Genesis 4:7). The Bible is full of what I call if/then statements: if we do this, then this happens. Or, if we don't do this, then this won't happen. Two things have become very clear to me about these rules: they work for everyone, and God doesn't bend them for anyone.

We have to have rules and laws in our society and God has sanctioned the governments of the world to make and enforce them. This is not to say the rules and laws are godly or that He necessarily agrees with them, but nonetheless, it's the system He allows. Rules are necessary. Consider what our world would be like if everyone simply did what he or she wanted. Chaos would reign and progress and productivity would be non-existent.

Our oldest daughter, who was recently released from prison for the fourth time, does not understand the concept of rules. This is the main error in thinking among all prisoners. For some reason, they feel the rules are not for them. Our daughter has been out such a short time, yet she is already slipping into the old behavior of not following rules. The house where she is living has definite rules: 8:00 pm curfew, home on weekends, attend meetings, etc. She thinks the rules are stupid and, consequently, ignores them. This behavior will eventually get her evicted and she will, once again, be on the downward spiral. I've tried explaining to her that relapse is never an event; it is always a process and begins with the little things, like breaking the rules. She knows this on an intellectual level, could even teach it, but somehow fails to see herself in it.

This daughter has never accepted rules and authority, even when she was a little girl. This is the reason she has four prison terms behind her. But she is no longer a little girl. She is a beautiful, intelligent, caring young woman who is fast approaching the 40-year-old mark. To say that she has not lived up to her potential would be a gross understatement. There's still time left, but not if she doesn't quit beating her head against the wall. God loves her unconditionally, but He's not going to change the rules for her.

*Then He said unto them, take heed and beware of
covetousness: for a man's life consisteth not in the
abundance of the things which he possesseth.*
Luke 12:15

We are a society that greatly values an abundance of
possessions: cars, boats, homes, power, and most of all,
money. But Jesus tells us very plainly in the above verse
that we are not to covet these things, for they are not the true
substance of life.

It's sad to watch people chase around after the abundance of "things" they believe they must have to achieve
happiness. I know, for I spent many years being one of
those people. I always had a good job and was considered
a prized employee wherever I worked. Before you become
too impressed, please understand that a prized employee is
nothing more than a person who does more than their share
of work, more than they're paid to do. I would go to work
for a company in a position I really liked and could handle
efficiently, and then promptly work myself silly to get a
promotion to a position I *didn't* like and, consequently, did
not excel at. I never once considered that I was happy doing
what I was originally hired to do. That was totally irrelevant.
Climbing the corporate ladder at any cost was the name of
the game.

Then there were the "things" I had to own. We had a
beautiful new house we built ourselves, a new boat, a nice
car, a nice truck, a daughter who wore designer clothes and
drove a new car, and 32 credit cards that were maxed out. I
even remember considering buying an airplane! And I was
drinking myself to death—literally. I was sure each new
"thing" was going to bring me the peace and joy I so desperately sought. Instead, they would just plunge me further into
despair and deeper into the pit of misery.

It was not until God reached down and pulled me out of that pit and I quit drinking, that I learned the meaning of true abundance. It didn't happen overnight. I had a lot of wrong thinking to overcome, but slowly I learned. We had to lose just about everything we had, file for bankruptcy, and go without work for eight months before God was able to get His truths through to me.

We have now re-established our credit, are financially stable, and have all that we need. There are no new houses, boats, or cars. We live in a company house. I drive an 8-year-old car and my husband drives a 10-year-old pickup, but we have untold abundance, peace, and joy.

*Then the Lord rained upon Sodom & Gomorrah brim-
stone and fire and He overthrew those cities and all the
inhabitants.*
Genesis 19: 24-25

With the exception of Lot and his family, God completely
destroyed the towns of Sodom and Gomorrah and all the
people within them. Why? Because of their totally immoral,
ungodly behavior. They were interested only in fulfilling
their own perverse pleasures, the greatest of which was
the widespread practice of homosexuality and other sexual
deviations.

"Sad," you say. "But they deserved it," you say. Well, if
that's your opinion, I invite you to pull your head out of the
sand and look around you.

At the present moment I'm in a lovely southern California
town where my husband is attending a two-day training class
for his job. After sight seeing yesterday, I returned to our
hotel to rest and wait for the dismissal of his class. I was
flipping through the television channels and was appalled at
some of the things I saw. I am not an avid television watcher
and was totally ignorant of the daytime talk shows.

I was both horrified and mesmerized by the content of
two of the shows I came across. On one, the host was inter-
viewing two sisters who obviously hated each other judging
by the slanderous remarks they were exchanging. It was
difficult to follow the actual conversation since at least every
other word was bleeped out, but not difficult to get the drift
of it. They both weighed about 350 pounds, but one of them,
fortunately, did have on clothes. The other one, however,
was prancing around in nothing but panties and a bra (a sight
that I'm afraid will be forever burned in my memory). The
whole object of the confrontation seemed to be that they
were both sleeping with the same guy and had just discovered it. I couldn't believe it.

The other show had a mother and her 14-year-old daughter. The mother was concerned about her daughter's activities and the daughter screamed at her, "Yes, I've had oral sex with more than 20 different guys and I don't always use protection. And yes, I do use drugs and not only that, I also sell them." Fourteen years old. Just a baby.

I wanted to fall to my knees and tell God, "I'm so sorry I belong to this human race." How sad He must be when He looks down on us. Perhaps we should keep a watchful eye on the heavens. The fire and brimstone may begin to rain on us at any moment just as it did on Sodom and Gomorrah.

Now I rejoice, not that ye were made sorry, but that ye sorrowed to repentance; for ye were made sorry after a godly manner...
2 Corinthians 7:9

Next to this verse in my Bible I have all three of our children's names written with various dates beside the names. Each date represents a difficult time in that child's life; a time when I have run to this scripture for comfort. Unfortunately, all the dates represent a time in their *adult* lives. If I had raised them by Biblical principles, I have no doubt their adult lives would be much smoother. Let me give you take a peek at the reality that *was* my children's raising instead of what it should have been.

I've come to believe there are two types of alcoholics; the saved and the unsaved. The unsaved alcoholic is able to drink with abandon, not caring who he hurts. He has no remorse and certainly no feeling of the need for repentance. He is often abusive and totally self-absorbed. I'm ashamed to admit, there was a time in my drinking years that I admired this person. I wanted to be able to drink without the guilt, the self-loathing, the condemnation. Ah, but alas, I was a saved alcoholic, and God simply wouldn't allow me the reckless, carefree drinking others seemed to enjoy.

So I lived in a constant state of guilt and remorse and sorrow and depression. In order to soothe that guilt and to ease some of the pain my children experienced because of me, I kept them from the sorrow and pain of their own mistakes. Consequences were not a concept I allowed them to learn. For instance, our oldest daughter who began a lifetime (so far) drug addiction at a very early age, seldom had to pay the full cost of her mistakes when she was a teenager. She would write hot checks, I would pick them up. She would go to jail, I would bail her out. She would get expelled from school, I would take her shopping. It was the same, in one form or another, for all my children. I was "protecting" them from the pain of the world.

In reality, what I was doing was teaching them they didn't have to be responsible for their own actions. They were all young adults by the time I went into recovery and discovered the errors in my thinking. It was difficult for them when they learned I was no longer going to be their rescuer. Each one of them has had to experience, on numerous occasions, the sorrow that leads to repentance. I'm grateful to say they *have* learned and do not hold it against me that they didn't learn it when they should have. We must allow people to suffer the sorrow that leads to repentance. Only then can God use their mistakes to better their lives.

*For ye have not received the spirit of bondage again to
fear...*
Romans 8:15

Bondage to what? I would guess that this verse is not talking about the type of slavery that Lincoln abolished in our country. Rather, I believe it is referring to bondage to anything except God that may have a hold on us: work, relationships, drugs, alcohol, possessions. I have been a slave to many things in my life, and I can say with certainty that slavery always leads to fear.

My longest term with bondage was the 32 years I spent chained to a bottle. Fear was my constant companion during that period. I was afraid I was an alcoholic (though I finally lost that fear when I came to realize there was no doubt that I was an alcoholic). I was afraid my husband and children didn't love me. I was afraid my life had no meaning. I was afraid of dying. And I was afraid of living. Once God helped me to escape that hell, all of the fears associated with my alcoholism left me almost immediately. I thought my life was going to be perfect. But then I began to see that my slavery to alcohol had been so all-encompassing that it masked many smaller issues that were also keeping me behind bars. There were numerous addictions; nicotine, caffeine, gambling, over-eating, impulsive spending, etc. Slowly, however, God has helped me to work on each of these fear-producing areas in my life.

Now I face a fear that I thought would never be a problem again. Our daughter, who was just recently released from prison, seems to be once again choosing the path that led her to incarceration four different times in the past. I find that I am still a slave to the dread that forms in a hard knot in the middle of my stomach when I can't get in touch with her. It practically paralyzes me with fear. The truth is, I am a slave to her actions.

I have spent much time in prayer over this. Just today, when people are calling the house because no one has seen her since yesterday morning, I am in a quandary as to how to handle it. I sensed God telling me earlier that as much as I love her, He loves her more and if He is unable to do anything with her free will, I sure can't. So how do I handle it? How should I feel? Is there *anything* I can do? At this moment, I don't have the answers to these questions. However, I know the One who does. As He delivered me from my other bondages, He will also free me from the slavery of this fear.

...that likewise joy shall be in heaven over one sinner that repenteth, more than over ninety and nine just persons, which need no repentance.
Luke 15:7

It was one of those enlightening moments, one of those "eurekas", when I realized that repentance and remorse are *not* interchangeable words. For years I thought I was repenting for the terrible things I was doing, when in truth all I was doing was suffering from remorse, and did I ever suffer.

Anyone who has ever engaged in heavy drinking for a prolonged period (I feel my 32 years qualifies as a prolonged period), understands what I mean about remorse and suffering. I would begin to wake each morning about 2:00 when the alcohol started to wear off and withdrawal set in (I learned in recovery that this is referred to as the midnight crazies). I always wanted to die, actually hoped that I would. My morning routine consisted of brushing my teeth, gagging, throwing up, drinking a cup of coffee, throwing up again, taking two aspirin, smoking a cigarette, and finally keeping down a cup of coffee. Then started the task of repairing the damage so that I would at least be presentable for work.

Every morning of my life was that way, and I would cry out to God to forgive me and to help me. I thought that was repentance, but it wasn't. Why didn't it qualify? Because I could hardly wait to get off work each day and start over again. Those of you who have never had a drinking problem will find it hard to understand doing that, knowing the scene I just described is going to take place the next morning. I don't understand it either. I *lived* it and I didn't understand it then and I don't understand it now.

My point is this: remorse is feeling bad physically or spiritually. But as soon as the bad feeling passes, the remorse is also gone, along with any righteous commitments that were made in the midst of the pain and agony.

Repentance, however, is a deep sorrow over an act or acts, a confession of the wrongdoing (if only to God), and a strong determination resulting in a permanent change of behavior. That is not to say the repentant person never slips back into the old ways. We are creatures of habit and old habits die hard. But the person serious about his repentance recognizes the slip for what it is, takes it once again to God, and picks himself up with a renewed determination. This is true repentance, the kind God works through with us, the kind that brings victory to our lives.

Do not be deceived; evil communications corrupt good manners.
1 Corinthians 15:33

Bracelets with the letters W.W.J.D. imprinted on them are very popular right now. The letters stand for "What Would Jesus Do?" The theory behind the bracelets is to remind the wearer every time he faces a decision or must make a choice to ask himself that question. It's an excellent idea. If everyone would stop and ask that very thing before going forward, the world would be such a different place. There would still be plenty of mistakes because the answer is not always clear, but life would certainly be sweeter.

I don't think I have become a prude in my old age, but I am appalled at the morality, or rather lack of it, in our country today. As my faith grows and I mature spiritually, I'm much easier offended than I was when I was out there in the middle of it.

Just look at the television shows (which I seldom do). They're filled with sex, promiscuity, fornication, adultery, and homosexuality. And those are just the sitcoms. The movies and other serial programs have all of these elements plus violence, murder, stealing, lying, cursing, and pure unhappiness. I do not understand why this is allowed or how it can be called entertainment. I know the industry's standard answer, "You don't have to watch if you don't like it." I consider that a copout. I *don't* watch, but my life is affected by the millions who do watch and then go out and imitate what they see. Those who wield such power concerning what enters the living rooms of this country should take it upon themselves to act in a responsible manner when planning programming. As bad as regular network television is, it makes me wonder what must be on the pay programming. But it is just an idle wonder I don't really want to know.

We moralists look at the young people today in their freaky clothes, with every conceivable body part either pierced or tattooed (or both) and their even more freaky behavior and determine that the world is going to hell in a hand basket. And maybe it is, but it is not these kids fault, no matter how relieved it would make us to be able to shift the responsibility to them. We've not only allowed them to come to this place by our desire, as parents, to just be left alone and not bothered, but we have given them a map showing them the way through our movies and TV shows, our own actions, and our apathy. W.W.J.D? Consider it.

Stone #2

Challenges

⌘

O thou of little faith, wherefore didst thou doubt?
Matthew 14:32

> *Now therefore go, and I will be with thy mouth, and*
> *teach thee what thou shalt say.*
> Exodus 4:12

God was talking to Moses after He had called him to lead the people from their Egyptian bondage into the Promised Land. Moses was giving God all the excuses why he couldn't do what God was ordering him to do. One of the reasons was that Moses did not feel he spoke well, *"O my Lord, I am not eloquent for I am slow of speech and of a slow tongue"* (Exodus 4:10). This prompted the above reply from God after reminding Moses that it was He, after all, who had made man's mouth in the first place.

I can relate to Moses. It seems every time I feel God calling me to something new, I immediately start coming up with reasons (excuses?) why it simply isn't possible. *I already have too much to do. I'm too old. I don't know how.* And the list goes on and on. I suppose I want to believe that God has forgotten how much I'm already doing. Or that He isn't aware of how old I am. Or that He doesn't know what my abilities are (like He didn't give them to me in the first place). Regardless of what I would like to think, the truth is He knows every tiny detail of my life and my circumstances and me *before* He ever calls. My excuses hold no more water than Moses' did.

When God called me to start writing seriously I was sure He had made a mistake. Yes, I know God doesn't make mistakes, but I thought I might be the exception to the rule—pretty egotistical, huh? Here came the excuses. *I'm an accountant, that's what I've done all my life. I'm too old to be changing careers. I don't know what to write. I don't know how to write.* And that was just the beginning.

I was new in my walk with God (not a new Christian, mind you, just new to the spiritual life), and wanted to be obedient. In spite of my objections, I came to a place of surrender relatively fast (there are some advantages to being impulsive!). God kept taking me to the above verse. He showed me that my responsibility was to go (*"Now therefore go "*). After that He steps in and the results are His responsibility. (*"and I will)*. So I did, and He did.

Has it always been easy? Certainly not. Read the story of Moses' 40-year trek through the wilderness with a million or so grumbling, complaining Israelites. God never once told him it would be easy, and He doesn't tell us it will be easy. But if we go, He does promise to be with us every step of the way and He does promise the calling will culminate in success and accomplishment.

*...and hath made of one blood all nations of men for to
dwell on all the face of the earth, and hath determined
the times before appointed, and the bounds of their
habitation...*
Acts 17:26

If I read this verse correctly, I'm in exactly the place at
exactly the time God intended. This is comforting since I
currently reside in a town that has one small general store
(prices out of sight and expiration dates long past), two
service stations, one post office, three casinos, and several
bars. I often say that my major goal in life is to live in a town
that has a grocery store — a real grocery store. It's funny how
the things we take so much for granted can become real luxuries when we have to do without them. Anyway, I'm glad to
know that God has appointed this place at this time for me.
Actually, I'm just glad to read that He even knows where I
am. Sometimes it's easy for me to forget that.

I'm going through a difficult time right now and a lot
of it has to do with our physical location. Our church is in a
town 75 miles away and I long to be closer to it and to my
friends within the church. In the past, I wasn't much of a
social person, preferring the company of my husband and
family. But that changed when I became actively involved
in our church and started making friends from within the
congregation. I had never had Christian friends before and
oh, how different they are from my drinking buddies who
inhabited my former life. These people care for me, they
love me, they laugh with me, they cry with me, and they
pray with me and for me. They are such a blessing and I want
to be able to develop a real social life with them, not just a
little time on Sunday and an occasional phone call. And the
church itself. Though I am involved in various activities, it's
not near to the extent I would like to be. I would like to be
there every time the door opened. (It's occurred to me on

more than one occasion that perhaps that is the very reason God has us living so far away, He knows I have trouble with balance in my life.)

Then there is the work thing. More and more I am feeling a desire to return to the work force. But, as it is easy to surmise from my description of the town, jobs are not exactly plentiful here unless I want to cashier or waitress. Please don't misunderstand, I'm certainly not putting down these professions. It's simply that I'm not trained to do either and they do not bring the money I would be seeking with re-employment. Once again, I wonder if this is a plus and another reason I'm here. For if I get completely honest with myself, which I just hate to have to do, I don't believe the desire to go to work is coming from God. I think that it stems more from wanting to run away from finishing this book He has commissioned me to write than run to a new job.

Most days I know I'm where God wants me to be even if I seldom understand the reason. My job is to be obedient His job is to produce results.

Children's children are the crown of old men...
Proverbs 17:6

As I write this, my husband and I are on our way to Las Vegas to the airport to pick up our oldest grandson and his girlfriend who are coming in for the weekend.

This grandson is 18 years old and a freshman in college. We have three other grandchildren: a 14-year old boy, a 12-year old boy, and a girl 5-years-old. This is the first time one of our grandchildren has ever been to see us. The 14-year-old we haven't seen in 7 years and the 5-year-old we haven't seen since she was 6 months old. Makes you wonder about our family, doesn't it? Well, none of our children have their children because of divorce, drug use, etc., and of course, those things are always lose/lose situations. No one wins, least of all the children and the grandparents, because they are the ones who may suffer the most but have the least to say about the situation.

The grandchild we are going to pick up today is very special. They are all special, but he was the first. He was born when I was 36 years old making me a grandmother at an age when many women are still having their own babies. Our daughter (his mother) was totally incapable of raising him, just being a baby herself and already five years into the drug scene. My husband and I couldn't take care of him. We both worked and were deep into our own alcoholic hell. But my mother and dad wanted him and now it shames me to think how readily we all consented to them taking him. However, God had his hand in it and it turned out to be the best thing that could have happened for our grandson, and, I might add, for my mother and dad.

My mother died earlier this year, her job with him completed. Now we all have the challenge of incorporating him into our family. I had not realized how isolated my mother kept him until she left us all to deal with the situation. He is actually coming this weekend to see his mother whom he has not seen in six years. The visit will take place inside the prison where she is currently incarcerated, but I see it as the beginning of a relationship between the two of them. At least that is my prayer. I admire his courage for coming. It is, I'm sure very difficult for them both.

This time of the year (the Christmas season) I always have the image of a lovely home in the snow-covered pines that is beautifully decorated for Christmas. There is smoke coming from the chimney, and the children drive up and the grandchildren pile out of the cars, filling the air with their laughter and excitement. That ideal will never be a reality for me and it will always be one of my greatest regrets.

*And he hath filled him with the Spirit of God, in
wisdom, in understanding, and in knowledge, and in
all manner of workmanship.*
Exodus 35:31

This verse refers to Bezaleel who was called to work as a
designer and engraver on the construction of the tabernacle
that God had ordered the Israelites to build. These verses, this
one and the ones surrounding it, fascinate me. God wanted
a tabernacle built and He was excruciatingly specific about
how it was to be done. His detailed instructions left no doubt
how the finished project would look right down to the clasps
on the curtains.

Why does it fascinate me? Because He didn't just throw a
set of blueprints at Moses and say, "Here's what I want, now
get your people together and figure out how you're going to
do it." No, He knew exactly what materials and skills would
be required for the completion. He filled the hearts of the
people with the know-how (wisdom, understanding, and
knowledge) of all the craftsmanship needed. Verse 34 tells
us He even filled Bezaleel with the desire to teach others
his craft. Further, it said Moses had to tell the people to quit
bringing contributions for the construction because they had
far more than they needed.

I wonder how many people miss the incredible joy and
blessings of following God's call on their lives because they
think they are not capable. When God called me out of a 35
year corporate America accounting career to set up a little
home office and start writing life-skills articles for prisoners,
I admit I thought I was standing in someone else's airwaves
and had picked up signals meant for another. I didn't have
anything required to do what He was calling me to do—not
the wisdom, the knowledge, the understanding, or the craftsmanship. I did, however, have the desire. He had already
been working on me in that area. So I was open for change

and He had even supplied me with enough faith to believe it was possible.

Afraid? Yes, there was fear, but He had also given me enough determination and sense of commitment to step out in spite of the fear. I'm not saying it's always been easy. He doesn't just zip us open and deposit everything we need then zip us closed (though I've always thought that was a lovely idea). We have to work to attain the skills we need. We have to hustle to pay the bills. We have to reach out to others and ask for help. But we can *always* be assured that everything we need to do that we're called to do is available to us, whether it be instruction, guidance, money, moral support, etc. It is our responsibility to find what we need and do whatever it takes to accomplish our calling.

*Fear thou not; for I am with thee: be not dismayed; for
I am thy God: I will strengthen thee...*
Isaiah 41:10

I have done something that I frequently regret. I prayed for God to relentlessly convict me of my overeating, overspending, and inconsistent time management habits. It's one of those prayers to which He's been so gracious to answer affirmatively. Right now I'm having a rough time with His yes answer, but I'm determined to stay with the prayer until there is no longer any need (which may not happen until I enter heaven but that's okay too).

For this writing, I will mention only the overeating since God has shown me that I'm not dealing with three separate issues as it appears, but only one. I have an idea that once I get the eating thing under control, the other two will fall into place.

Let me clarify something. I am not grossly overweight. I'm only talking about 10 or 15 pounds, but I absolutely believe it is not the number that is important. I could feel no worse about myself and my sin of gluttony if the issue was 100 pounds or 200 pounds. I believe the concept is the same no matter what the number. And it's not about food, just as overspending is not about money. It is about self-esteem, self-confidence, discipline, determination, persistence, commitment, and ultimately, obedience to God.

I've tried many methods of weight loss. They all worked. For me, losing the weight, though a challenge, is not a major problem (however, since I've hit that magic half-century mark, it is not near as easy as it once was). No, my problem is keeping it off once I've lost it. That's why I was so excited about the last program I followed. It is based on Biblical principles and it does not focus on food or dieting, but encourages the development of totally new lifetime eating habits.

I still believe in the program. I lost 15 pounds over a period of several months, but slowly reverted back to my old eating habits: too much, too often, too many sweets. I've mistakenly been looking at the program as just one more failure in a long line of failures. The program didn't fail. It was a huge success. I failed when I quit following it. But as I often say, "Failure is an event, not a person."

As I was thinking about the situation, God led me to the above verse. I've been looking at my circumstances and at the ten pounds I've regained, and have been telling myself that I will never be able to succeed. And on my own, which is how I've attacked it in the past, I can't do it. My focus must be on Him. He will strengthen me. Yes, I will still have to exercise self-control and say no to the chocolate cake. However, the strength to do that will not have to come from me, but it will come from Him.

Jesus answered and said unto him, "If a man love me, he will keep my words: and my Father will love him, and we will come unto him and make our abode with him."
John 14:23

What an awesome thought, Jesus and the Father making their abode (home) with me. Is my home in order? Is it a suitable residing place for such holy Residents? Probably not, but nonetheless, that is what and where They are.

Our oldest daughter, who is currently in prison, told me one day that when she returned to her room (cell) from work, she looked around at her chest, her books, and her Bible, and decided she wouldn't mind at all if Jesus Himself walked in. At the time I thought that was a very strange thing for her to think about. But now I believe it is something we all should consider.

Would I mind if Jesus, in the flesh, walked into my house? I believe I can truthfully say no, I wouldn't mind. I have nothing to hide and it's even reasonably clean and organized. It has not always been that way. There was a time I would have been ashamed for my earthly father to walk unannounced into my house much less my heavenly Father. Oh, it was always pretty clean, but there were so many secrets (not the least of which were vodka bottles hidden everywhere). In those days an unexpected visit from anyone was cause for incredible stress. It makes me so sad now to know how my life must have grieved my heavenly Father.

The mind, which is also the abode of God and His Son has been a little more difficult for me to clean up than my outward home. Satan attacks each of us differently depending on our vulnerable areas. For some he attacks their circumstances. I've got a relatively good attitude about circumstances and changes in them for the good or bad affect me little. He pretty much leaves me alone in that area. My mind is where he sets up shop and does his best work on me.

My powers of concentration are weak and I'm ashamed of my seeming inability to even get through a prayer without my mind straying to the most unimportant things. I say "seeming inability" because I know that it only appears that way. God would not have commanded us in His Word to pray if we didn't have the ability to do it. Though I don't like to admit it, I know it's only laziness on my part. Focus and concentration are hard work. But if I want God's abode to be fit for Him, I must constantly work at cleaning and improving it.

Jesus said unto him, If thou canst believe, all things
are possible to him that believeth.
Mark 9:23

This is a direct quote from Jesus. All things are possible to him who believes what? To him who believes that all things are possible. I think this is one of God's natural laws, one of those principles that works for the saved as well as the unsaved. Could I, by believing it is possible, go out and rob a bank. Yes, if I believed it strongly enough to put in the necessary time, effort, and risk (I must always remember that there is a certain risk and there are consequences associated with every action). So yes, I could rob a bank if I believed I could.

God, however, set His principles in motion for His children. Though the unsaved can also practice them with a certain amount of outward success, it is the true believers who reap the blessings that accompany the promises.

Is there an obligation or responsibility on my part that must be fulfilled in order for me to claim the promises? Absolutely! Every promise of God comes with a string attached. In the case of this one, I must believe that all things are possible. Especially those things God calls me to—those things that in the see, feel, hear, taste, smell, touch world seem impossible. Those things that, without divine intervention from God, are impossible.

I've had many such things in my life; many before I was even aware of God's presence. He kept and protected me through childhood sexual abuse and kept me from the resentment and bitterness that follows that type of thing. He kept my husband and I together through 30 years of drinking and incredible unhappiness, bringing us into a place of love and joy. He protected our children through their growing-up years when they had neither the environment nor the parents that all children deserve.

If God can perform these monumental feats without my conscious awareness, why in the world would I ever limit Him in the realm of impossibility? When I look at something such as having a book published, losing and keeping off 15 pounds, or becoming a public speaker and say, "That's impossible," I'm limiting God. I'm looking at my own strengths and abilities and in that case, I'm correct. Those accomplishments are impossible for me. But it just so happens, those are a few of the things to which He has called me so I must remember the above verse as I embark on them.

...the Lord will receive my prayer.
Psalm 6:9

I teach a discipleship training class on prayer at our church's Sunday morning Bible study hour. Well, maybe teach is not the appropriate word since I have probably learned more than the rest of the class. What I do is guide us through the course.

Prayer has always been, and still is, a difficult area for me. I'm never satisfied with my prayers and I feel I never pray exactly right. Like everything else, I complicate the process. I don't believe God intends for us to do that.

In Luke 11:1, Jesus' disciples requested, *"Lord, teach us to pray "*His response to them was what has become known as "The Lord's Prayer." It is beautiful in its simplicity, yet covers every aspect of life. It begins by acknowledging God and His holiness. It asks for provision for today (note for today only, not tomorrow or next week). It asks for forgiveness of our sins and help that we may forgive others. It asks for help in resisting Satan's attacks. It ends by, once again, acknowledging God's holiness and power. This is Jesus' own instruction in prayer. What could be simpler?

Why do I have such a problem with prayer? Well, there's my family. It's obvious I don't always know what's best for them or I wouldn't have made such a mess raising my children, so how do I pray for them? And what about my extended family? Due to sporadic contact, I seldom even know what's going on in their lives. Yet, I feel the obligation to pray for them.

Paul tells us throughout the Epistles that we are to pray for our church leaders. How do I know what they need beyond the strength, courage, and wisdom needed to continue in their roles? And what about our government leaders whom we are also instructed to pray? There is so much need there that I hardly know where to start.

The Bible tells me I have a responsibility to pray, so I work my way through it. Some days it goes well and I feel very close to God during my prayer time. Other days it seems nothing more than a chore and I'm filled with guilt, not only concerning the prayer itself, but my feelings that are connected to the prayer. It's obvious my calling is not to be a prayer warrior. However, I do strive to become an effective, fervent pray-er who can accomplish much (James 5:16).

The one who calls you is faithful and he will do it.
1 Thessalonians 5:24

I have a pretty simple formula for knowing if I'm in God's will in a certain thing. If it goes smoothly and I have peace, it's God's will. If, on the other hand, I'm in constant frustration, nothing works, and my interest wanes early, well, it's not God's will. That's not to say being in His will is assurance of a carefree walk with no trials, tribulations, pain, or disappointments. After all, look at Jesus. He was *always* in God's perfect will and people rejected Him, betrayed Him, used Him, beat Him, and spat on Him. His journey on the path of God's will finally took Him to the cross and an agonizing death.

No, if you're expecting easy, I can't recommend heeding God's call. But if you're looking for a simple, exciting, and fulfilling life beyond comprehension, then it's the only way to go. And if you stick with it, you can be certain that God's will in your life will come to pass in His perfect timing. But there has to be a total surrender to His way, a commitment to immediate obedience, and a determination to stick with it when you don't see anything happening.

At one time God called me to write a monthly self-help motivational publication for prison inmates. I was sitting at a red light on my way to my accounting job when the call came. Though I was sure I misunderstood, I couldn't deny it. The call was clear. How could I possibly do that? I was an accountant. I knew nothing about writing, publishing, prison systems, etc. On my own, I *couldn't* do it. But as the above verse says, when He calls, He accomplishes.

I was sure that since my venture was mandated by Him that it would be an instant success. You would think that, right? Wrong. Just because He was ready for me to start didn't mean I knew all there was to know. There was much work—deep work to be done within me before I would be ready for success. For one thing, I was still caught up in a gambling addiction at the time. Monetary success in my business could have driven me to the brink of destruction. I had to gain victory over that (and I'm grateful to report that God delivered me from it shortly thereafter). I had to learn to become the type of person who is a success. Not an easy task for God to undertake. But He was up to the challenge and we've been working diligently on me in this area for the last several years.

Answer when God calls, but be willing to let *Him* bring it to pass, no matter what that may involve.

Neither give place to the devil.
Ephesians 4:27

Nice short verse. Easy to understand. To the point. How many words could possibly be written about it? Volumes. Many have the mistaken idea that if they don't run out and join a cult, or don ski masks and rob a bank, or run off with the neighbor's wife, they're pretty safe from the attacks of Satan. Wrong.

Actually, Satan never even tempts me with those things. Now, if I had a fascination with the charismatic leaders of the cults, or a propensity for illicit romantic entanglements, or a criminal mind, perhaps I would be lured by those possibilities. But I don't and I'm not. And Satan seldom tempts me in the areas that have been major problems for me in the past. For instance, I'm never tempted to take a drink, or to pick up a package of cigarettes. That's not to say I don't occasionally think about these things, but I don't entertain the thoughts; I don't sit down and fellowship with them. They are not areas of temptation for me. No, Satan doesn't mess with the big obvious frontal attacks. He's much more subtle and dangles other carrots in front of me. What kinds? Glad you asked.

A big beautiful piece of double fudge chocolate cake is nearly impossible for me to sidestep. Or a medium rare New York steak with a baked potato swimming in butter and sour cream. Or putting off that writing assignment until I'm down to the wire and can't give it the time and attention it deserves. Or giving in to the impulse to spend money on something I can't afford and don't even need. Or not shutting my mouth and letting that tacky remark escape and hurt another. Or withholding something that could be a blessing to another just because I don't want to take the time or the effort to offer it. Need I go on, or do you get the idea?

You may think the little things are not that important. After all, in the big scheme of things, just how important is a piece of chocolate cake? Actually, very important. Especially when there has been a commitment made to not defile the body with an abundance of sugar. If I allow Satan to tell me, "go ahead, just one piece is not going to make a difference," soon it's one, then another. Before long, I've lost my self-confidence, my self-esteem, and I hate myself, thinking I'll never be successful at weight loss. Then I throw away the whole program and lose my witness which is, of course, what he wanted in the first place.

Satan has a personalized plan to keep us in a constant state of struggle. We better have a plan of counter-attack.

To every thing there is a season, and a time to every
purpose under the heaven...
Ecclesiastes 3:1

This chapter in Ecclesiastes goes on to say that there's a time to be born and a time to die, a time to plant and a time to pluck up, a time to kill and a time to heal, a time to build up and a time to tear down, a time to weep and a time to laugh, a time to mourn and a time to dance, a time to cast away and a time to gather together, a time to be silent and a time to speak, a time to love and a time to hate, a time for war and a time for peace.

Obviously, nothing except God is forever. He's been dealing with me concerning this chapter for a couple of weeks now. I remember when my dad died and my mother left it to me as to what would be engraved on his headstone. After much deliberation, or as much deliberation as was possible at the time since I was still drinking, I decided on the above verse, *"To every thing there is a season."* The reason I chose this is because my dad, unlike anyone I had ever known, was able to accept the changing seasons of life without struggle or regret. My husband has since grown into that kind of person also. Now I'm blessed to have had two such people in my life. The ability to live life in such a manner is a rare gift and one that I envy and aspire to.

How do we know when the appropriate time is for something? For some, such as my dad and my husband, there seems to be a natural instinct. For the rest of us (the majority), I suppose it's a combination of trial and error and a whole lot of guidance from God. Now that I think about it, isn't guidance from God what natural instinct is also?

My challenge in this area is different from the challenge many have. Usually people start things and then give up too easily. My problem is turning loose when something is over — when God is finished with it. But I'm learning, and as always when He's teaching me something, there are lots of real-life practical examples to go to school on. This one is no exception.

We recently moved from one house to another. A matter in which we had no choice since we live in company housing. I balked at turning loose of what we had, but our time there was finished and what we came to, though not apparent at first, is much better. Now I'm feeling it's time to let go of the publication I've been writing for five years. It's not an easy decision, but God's grace has lifted from it, which is always an indication that it's time to let go. Mother Teresa said, "I always hold things lightly because it hurts too much when God has to pry them from my fingers." Help me, God, to know when to hold on and when to let go.

For Brethren, ye have been called unto liberty; only
use not liberty for an occasion to the flesh...
Galatians 5:13

I have an addictive personality as some of you may have gathered by now. If I like something, I have only to engage in it once for it to become an addiction. If I don't like it, it may take several times before the addiction kicks in but kick in it will. Consequently, it seems I am constantly seeking balance in my life and attaining that balance is my greatest challenge.

When Jesus came to earth and died for our sins, we were set free from the burden of the law. This is the freedom Paul refers to in the above verse. I don't do well with freedom. I have a fairly strict routine for those things I must do to keep myself sane. These include a stringent exercise program, carefully watching what I eat, daily writing, and regular time with God. As long as I do these on a daily basis, I'm okay with myself and happy with the world.

But what about those times when I can't perform one of these rituals? For instance, last Friday we had to take a trip that meant leaving home at 3:30 a.m. Needless to say, I found it unreasonable to get up early enough to get in my hour of morning exercise. For a "normal" person, this wouldn't have been a problem. Miss one day exercising, no big deal. But remember me, the addictive "all or nothing" personality, no semblance of normalcy.

Instead of doing what I could and dismissing what I couldn't, I threw it *all* overboard. I ate too much, didn't do my writing or reading (both of which could have been accomplished in the car), spent too much money, etc. In other words, as Paul warned against, I turned my freedom into an opportunity for the flesh.

The strange thing about these situations (no, last weekend was certainly not the first time this happened) is they not only don't bring me any pleasure, they cause remorse and self-loathing. And I know they don't please my Lord, which makes me sad.

As I was writing this and wondering why I do these things, God gave me the answer. It is a lack of self-control and self-discipline brought about my immaturity. Just like a little kid, my flesh says, *I don't really want to do this. I know it's going to bring me pain, but because I have the freedom, I'm going forward with it.* The solution? Ask God to grow me up and allow Him the freedom to do it.

*...one day is with the Lord as a thousand years, and a
thousand years as one day.*
2 Peter 3:8

Time is relative. If I'm spending the day in Las Vegas
with my husband, running errands, eating out, going to the
movies, and having fun, time passes much too fast. Before
I know it, it's time to come home. If we're on a three-day
camping trip, it seems we hardly get all of our gear unpacked
before it's time to re-pack and head for home. If I'm facing a
writing deadline and the words won't come, time melts away
as fast as a snow cone on a July afternoon.

On the other hand, if I'm sitting in my doctor's exam
room with nothing on but a paper gown (open in the front)
staring at the cold metal stirrups mounted on the end of the
table, time stands completely still. Or if I'm waiting by the
phone for my daughter to call with the results of a pregnancy
test, it seems the clock is running backwards. Or try sitting
in a courtroom while the judge deliberates the sentence he's
going to pass on your child.

Time *is* relative. And it is also a great equalizer. Each of
us has 24 hours in our day, no more, no less. Bill Gates may
have 12 billion dollars, but he only has the same 24 hours in
his day that I have in mine.

Why is it some people accomplish so much more with
their time than others do? It has to do with discipline and
time management. Time management, by the way, is a big
business right now. Books are written about it and courses
abound teaching the finer aspects of it. I considered, at
one time, taking a class offered by a company which was
marketing a planner (that's calendar to you unsophisticated
types). The course taught a system to use the planner efficiently. I decided against it when I realized the cost (several
hundred dollars), the length of the class (three days), and the

amount of time it was going to take me each day just to *plan* my day.

God's been dealing with me about managing my time but I don't think He necessarily wants me to attend classes to learn about it. I feel there's a lot He has for me to do and that means spending my time doing the important things and staying away from the "busy" work. It's the 80/20 rule in effect. Generally speaking, 80% of our productivity results from 20% of our efforts. The key to greater effectiveness is raising that productive effort rate.

I wasted a lot of years. I don't want to waste any more of the precious moments God grants me. And when I'm tempted to think I don't have enough time left to do anything significant for God, I'm reminded of the above verse.

...for I have learned, in whatsoever state I am, there-
with to be content.
Philippians 4:11

I read a story about a man who was reflecting on his life as he drove to work. He and his wife had argued that morning, and his departure from home had been silent and sullen. One of his children was doing badly in school and the other was proving to be a real discipline problem. He enjoyed his job, but frequently felt he wasn't living up to his true potential. As he lamented over these various obstacles, he cried out to God to smooth out the problems so he get to what he perceived as the "good life." In the silence that followed his pleading prayer, he felt God speak to him, "This *is* your life."

This story was brought to my mind by a conversation with our daughter who was about to be released from prison. She said that all her life she has supposed she will be happy "when." When she finally gets off drugs for good. When she is released from prison and gets her name out of the legal system. When she finds the right man to love. And on and on and on. She said that God had revealed to her that morning as she sat outside with her coffee, that this is it. If she couldn't be happy at that moment, where she sat in the middle of a prison yard, it simply will never happen. She had her "aha" moment and it filled her with joy.

The same flash of insight happened for me this morning. I can't truthfully say it filled me with joy, but it did bring a certain amount of acceptance, and with that always comes peace. The revelation was brought on by my ever-present remorse concerning my seeming inability to bring my compulsive eating and overspending under control. As I sat with God in my early morning quiet time, I was trying to explain to Him that if He would just take care of these two things, my life would be perfect and I would never ask Him for anything else. I 'm sure there are times when I must be a great source of amusement to Him. I could feel Him saying, "Kay, Kay, Kay, I've given you everything you need to gain victory in these areas and I will be with you every step of the way, but I will not do it for you." And then I realized that when I have these challenges conquered, and I will, there will be something new to tackle. After all this is my life.

> *What? Know ye not that your body is the temple of the
> Holy Ghost which is in you, which ye have of God, and
> ye are not your own?*
> 1 Corinthians 6:19

This is certainly a thought-provoking question from
Paul. Kind of blows away the attitude, "Well, it's *my* body. I
can do whatever I want with it or to it." Verse 20 that follows
goes on to tell us that we were bought with a price (the life of
Jesus) and that we are to therefore glorify God in our body.

I look at my body most mornings as I emerge from the
shower (why would *anyone* place a mirror where this is even
possible?) and hardly see anything that would even remotely
glorify God. However, I realize now that the above verse
tells me I have a responsibility and an obligation to do whatever can be done to heed this high call.

I'm in no way talking about those physical attributes that
we can do nothing about. God is well aware of the too long
nose, the receding hairline, the limb that was lost in an accident, the paralysis that necessitates a wheelchair, the arthritis
that deforms the hands, the birthmark that covers half the
face, the scars from the fire, etc. No, these are not the things
that the verse is addressing. Keep in mind, though, that if
you have any of these or other seeming negative qualities,
they can definitely be used to glorify God. But that's another
subject for another time. For now we are discussing those
things that *are* within our control.

As you read through this book, you will realize why the
first thing that comes to my mind is overeating. Many will say
that what or how much they eat is not anyone's business. Not
true according to this verse. Let's face it, gluttony resulting
in extra weight is not only unhealthy, it certainly doesn't
glorify God. And what about addictions? Alcoholism, drugs,
sex, pornography, nicotine, gambling, and on and on the list
goes. Think what you do in the privacy of your own home

doesn't hurt anyone? Wrong. There is no way a person can engage in any of these activities without it affecting every part of his life. And besides, this verse tells us that the Holy Spirit is in us (those of us who are born again, that is). How can we do anything in absolute secret? We can't.

I am of the opinion that not taking care of ourselves is a highly selfish act. Though truly miraculous, the body is not indestructible. If it is abused long enough, it will eventually begin to break down. When that happens, someone has to step in and take care of that person who is no longer able to take care of himself. See the selfishness? Begin to see your body for what it is—a temple for the Holy Spirit, the very Spirit of God Himself. That should be a great motivation to begin to take care of it and treat it with the proper respect.

Wherefore, receive ye one another, just as Christ also
received us
Romans 15:7

Acceptance is an appropriate topic as I sit in the lobby of the prison where my lovely daughter currently resides while the rest of my family visits with her. My visitation privileges are tied up in bureaucratic red tape. But I accept this because it was through my own error that the problem was created.

Acceptance is a difficult concept to learn and to practice. At least it is for me. I have probably repeated the Serenity Prayer thousands of time since entering recovery. It goes like this, "God, grant me the serenity to accept the things I cannot change, the courage to change the things I can, and the wisdom to know the difference." My biggest need is the wisdom to know the difference. I'm always afraid I'm accepting the things I should be changing and am trying to change the things I should be accepting. I'm sure that, on occasion, I err on both. I just have to leave it to God to let me know in which area I should be operating.

A large portion of the Bible requires acceptance on my part because I don't understand it. Fortunately, though, God is granting me more and more understanding of His word and I believe it is because of my willingness to accept it *all* based on my faith in Him.

My past is one thing that has required a great deal of acceptance and I have accomplished that acceptance, nearly 100%. Wallowing in self-pity or living in regret over the past is the most negative non-productive use of time I know of. It's sad the number of people who waste the precious moments of the present doing just that.

I do spend a lot of time speaking and writing about all the negative aspects of my past. However, it is not done out of remorse or regret, but for the purpose of helping others who have been or are currently going through the same types of things. I figure God allowed me to live that wretched life for some reason; using my life to help others gives some positive meaning to it. I'm grateful for the opportunity.

I spent a lot of my life trying to change things I should have been accepting, which was mostly other people. We can never change another person. Actually, it's presumptuous on our part to even think we have a right to try. We need to accept others as they are and live in such a way ourselves that they are influenced by our behavior. Perhaps then they will desire to change the things within themselves that need to be changed. From there we let God handle it.

...whatsoever things are honest think on these things.
Philippians 4:8

Walter Lippman, writer, journalist, and political commentator, said, "A man has honor if he holds himself to an ideal of conduct though it is inconvenient, unprofitable, or dangerous to do." Based on this definition of honor (which I agree with), I've known very few people in my personal life who have possessed it. Most certainly, I myself have fallen far short of meeting the requirements.

I guess the closest to an honorable person I've had in my family was my mother. Though a lot of her ideas and values were pretty screwy in my estimation, she adhered to them with the tenacity of a bulldog. I believe her highest priority as far as values were concerned was honesty. That was most unfortunate too, as most of her family were hopeless liars. She, however, was the only person I've ever known that I could absolutely stand firm on *anything* that she told me. There is a great security in that. Of course, that was only true after she quit drinking. Everyone knows drinkers are totally unreliable in anything they do or say.

I want so much to be a person of honor. Calvin Coolidge, thirtieth President of the United States, said, "No person was ever honored for what he received. Honor has been the reward for what he gave." I want to be honored (or at least remembered) for what I gave. What kinds of giving?

First and foremost, I want to be remembered for the love I give. Love to my family. Love to the homeless. Love to the imprisoned. Love to my friends. But most of all, love to my God. I want to be honored for my unselfishness. I want to be a great channel, not a bottleneck, for God's blessings. I wish for His goodness to flow *through* me, in and then immediately out to others. I don't want to be guilty of hoarding anything and I never want things to be more important to me than people.

I want to be remembered for the gifts and talents God has so graciously bestowed upon me. I want it to be said I worked hard to develop them and used them to serve others and always gave God the glory. I want to leave books, articles, journals, letters, and notes that others will find helpful and uplifting for generations to come.

Does all of this sound selfish and self-centered? Perhaps it is, but I am only being honest. And I have a feeling I'm voicing the wishes of many people. Is what I have described possible? Certainly it is if I'm willing to do the work necessary to attain the honors. Am I willing? I'm not sure, but I know I'm closer to being willing now than I've ever been.

*For I Know the thoughts that I think toward you, saith
the Lord, thoughts of peace, and not of evil, to give you
an expected end.*
Jeremiah 29:11

When God said this to Jeremiah, He was talking about
the Jews who were in exile in Babylon. But I believe He has
the same message for everyone. Am I saying that I believe
God has an *individual* plan for each and every one of us?
Absolutely. I know, just the shear logistics of making twelve
billion plus (the approximate number of people that have
lived since time began) plans pretty much boggles the mind.
But remember, we're talking God here, the same God who
knows the name of each and every star.

I've always maintained that if everyone would operate
within God's will, using the talents and gifts God has
bestowed on each of us, the world would function in perfect
order and we could already be with Jesus enjoying heaven.
So why don't we? Well, it's that free will thing. God is not
going to force His will on us. And we, in all our infinite
wisdom, do not see the necessity of seeking His will. After
all, we already know what's best for us and what we do is
right in our own eyes (Proverbs 21:2).

I spent 35 years working as an accountant. It didn't bring
me a lot of joy and satisfaction and it did little to help anyone
else, but I hardly considered that relevant. I discovered at 18
years old that I had a natural aptitude for numbers. There was
a job opening requiring it, and I needed a job. With nothing
more than that, I got caught up in a 35 year career. It never
occurred to me to wonder if it was "right" for me or if it was
what God planned for me. For most of those 35 years I was
drinking anyway, so being out of God's will in one more area
would not have come as a shock.

After I had been sober for a few years and was learning
to tune my mind and my heart to God's, I began to feel

Him pulling me towards writing. I've now totally given up accounting (having nothing more than a hand held calculator for balancing my checkbook) and am into writing full-time. I love my work. It brings me untold joy and blessings.

The sad part of this story is the 35 years of joy and blessings I missed by not seeking God's will and developing the talent He gave me. But, as we all know, hindsight is 20/20 vision and I do not waste time with regrets. I simply allow the past to work within me a sense of urgency to not waste one precious moment I have left, but to use every one living in the perfect will of God as best I can.

God does have a plan for our lives. Just because we may not have started out in it does not mean we cannot finish in it. He will bring together all our errors in our walk and work them for the good (Romans 8:28).

> *But Daniel made up his mind to not defile himself with*
> *the king's choice food and the wine which he drank.*
> Daniel 1:8

This is a memory verse from my eating program. God brought my attention to my eating, overspending, and inconsistent work habits in one swoop. I went through several different emotions when I realized He was going to have me dealing with three uglies at the same time. These were not little minor personality flaws, but major character defects.

At first I patted myself on the back, assuming I must be growing into super spiritual maturity for Him to consider me to be in a position to work on all three of them. That is, until I actually started to work on them, at which time I went into my whiney mode with the mantra, "This is too much, God. Let's work on them one at a time. I can't do them all now."

That was when I felt that God was saying to me, "They aren't three, they are one." His messages and revelations to me are always short and simple. I would have liked some kind of explanation. It sure looked like three to me, but no explanation was forthcoming. Experience had told me, however, that I could trust that it was true, even if it made no sense.

I decided to give up the struggling, complaining, and whining, and just do what I knew to do. A large part of what I knew to do was just what the above verse states: make up my mind to not defile myself with overeating, overspending, and wasted work hours. It was simple enough though it wasn't always easy (easy and simple are two different things), but God had put a fiery determination in me and I got up after each fall with a new persistence.

Working with these three things gradually became easier. Then one morning I had one of those "aha" experiences, and God's message became clear. I wasn't dealing with eating, or money, or poor time management. It was all about self-discipline. The same principle for overcoming worked with all of them. It truly was only one issue, not three (imagine that, God was right). And what was the principle? Just as Daniel discovered: make up my mind to not defile myself.

Changing our lives is as simple as changing our minds. Our mind is where the battle takes place, not in our circumstances. We have but to make a decision to do what's right, then call on the strength God has already reserved for us to follow through on the decision. And should we stumble and fall? Then we allow God to reach down, pick us up, and give us a fresh supply of motivation and determination.

*For though we walk in the flesh, we do not war after
the flesh...*
2 Corinthians 10:3

Well, this verse could be pretty confusing. It is, however,
very clear to those of us who have ever been engaged in
spiritual warfare (which is any person who is serious about
their walk with God).

I am currently emerging from what I call a "valley walking
period." I used to think there was something wrong with me
because I experienced these times. However, I have since
learned that every Christian goes through them. So what is
"valley walking" like for me? It's a period of time when God
seems far away. My joy dims and I have difficulty remaining
optimistic. I can't muster enthusiasm for my prayers or my
Bible study. I want to eat everything in sight and forget the
exercise. Words are hard to come by and interest in writing
wanes. In short, my attitude leaves a lot to be desired.

In the past, I have given into these feelings. I stopped
doing what keeps me sane (exercise, prayer, Bible reading,
etc.) and given into the feelings of lethargy, discontent, and
general tackiness. The result? A growing consciousness of
self-loathing and magnified feelings of unhappiness that
seem to last forever. Even when I would finally emerge on
the far side of the valley, it would take a long time to get
back into the routine of my "sanity" activities and regain my
self-esteem, (the two are definitely connected for me).

Fortunately, I've allowed God to work with me through
these times and I no longer "throw the baby out with the bath
water." I can't pretend to know why we have these periods,
but I do know they are inevitable. I also know Satan will try
to use them if we allow him to. As the above verse says, we
are not battling our circumstances. When I go through one of
these periods I can never point to something tangible and say,
"This is the reason," and when I can't find a reason, Satan

goes to work on my mind. That is where the real battlefield is. But I've learned some warfare of my own, with God's help.

I no longer sit around and eat my way through my pity. I accept that it's not going to be a particularly creative time, so I set aside all but the most basic writing. I go to work on the menial jobs which, at other times, seem boring; those which have to be done but don't require much thought. And most importantly, I keep up my exercise, prayer, and Bible reading. Once I started doing this, I discovered these down periods are shorter in duration and less severe in intensity. The trick is to keep my focus on God and don't give in to Satan.

...and I will rebuild its ruins, and I will restore it.
Acts 15:16

I'm not sure what ruin is—in man, at least. Concerning material things, ruin can be very obvious. If I spill red Kool-Aid on my white silk blouse, it is obviously ruined. Or is it? Perhaps with a little professional touch my white silk blouse could become my new black silk blouse. There are the ruins in Athens, which are nothing more than the remains of buildings and coliseums from hundreds and hundreds of years ago. But even they are not ruins in the true definition of the word, for now they serve the purpose of a tourist attraction which puts us in touch with our ancient history. So perhaps material things are never ruined, just changed in appearance or purpose. And maybe the same is true of people who think they are "ruined" by circumstances.

Because of my business, I am in frequent contact with prisoners, both by letter and in person. Now you would think that being in prison would be a valid reason for a person to think his or her life is ruined. Especially those facing sentences that will encompass a good portion of their lives. And it's true that many do feel that way. They are the ones who are easy to spot. They act like tough guys who wouldn't be caught dead in a seminar, library, or chapel. They've never read a book and their talk is liberally sprinkled with four-letter expletives. They have no visitors and profess to prefer it that way. And true to their beliefs, their lives *are* often ruined, and change is not a great possibility for them.

The other side of that coin, however, houses a high percentage of prisoners. They are the ones who may have spent some time in the beginning feeling sorry for themselves, but then they picked themselves up by their own boot straps (not an easy feat in case you've never tried it) and decided to make the most of the situation. Needless to say, these are the people I hear from. This group is also easy to spot. They are enthusiastic and their eyes shine with hope and faith. You will seldom see them in front of the TV or at a card game. They have a book under their arm everywhere they go (often times it is the Bible) and are voracious readers. They are sitting in every group and seminar offered and attend church services regularly. They work hard to make amends with their families and rebuild damaged relationships. Ruined lives? These people will tell you that going to prison was the best thing that ever happened to them.

Ruined is a relative term. If we will take our "ruins" and turn them over to God and allow Him to work with us, we will see our ruins turned into incredible miracles.

Stone #3

Change

Because they have no changes, therefore they fear
not God.
Psalm 55:19

I am debtor both to the Greeks, and to the Barbarians;
both to the wise, and to the unwise.
Romans 1:14

When God pulled me from that awful pit of self-destruction called alcoholism, I selfishly thought it was solely for my own benefit. To some extent, it was for me. I was His child, though, as the popular saying goes, had they been convicting Christians, there wouldn't have been enough evidence to even arraign me. But he didn't want to see me suffer through the slow agonizing death I was inflicting on myself.

For several years He pampered me with His love and His care. He allowed me to work through the living problems that caused my drinking and were caused by my drinking. He motivated me to bring my physical condition and my mental facilities up to an acceptable level. I can't say I was always gung-ho about this complete make-over. Sometimes I would balk. Often I would procrastinate. He allowed me a little leeway occasionally, but mostly He would stay right in my face, pulling me forward. It eventually got easier when I realized that all I had to do was look at my past then I would be more than happy to stay on His path of reformation.

As I advanced through the years of my recovery, I was sure I would reach the place where I was "fixed" of all my character defects and could sit back and really enjoy the good life. After all, wasn't that the reason he had delivered me from my alcoholism and the myriad of other addictions that had always plagued me? Surely it was so I could tiptoe through the tulips in the sunshine with a light heart and an untroubled mind. Well, not exactly.

I started getting strange urges. Volunteer at the local drug treatment center. Change majors in my college work from accounting to psychology. Start to write about some of my experiences. Quit my job and write a self-help publication for prisoners (that was a biggie). Give basic life skill presentations to the homeless and to ex-offenders. Volunteer to take over the church newsletter. Start to teach a Sunday School class. What was all of this? Where did it come from? What about my carefree, sun-filled days?

That was when I came across the above verse and realized what was happening. Like Paul, God had delivered me from a wretched life. And like Paul, I now have a responsibility. God wants me to minister to those who suffer with the same afflictions I had. He wants me to stand as an example that there is hope for their lives, that what He did for me He will do for them. I have an obligation. And if God has done anything at all for you, you have an obligation too.

All the days of my appointed time will I wait, till my change comes.
Job 14:14

One of the main things I learned early in recovery is that one person cannot change another person. Reformation is an inside job whether it is a person, a family, a church, a community, a nation, or the world. Outside forces may be useful for influence, guidance, and direction, but ultimately, the change must come from within and it must be preceded by a burning desire for that change, which, I believe, God supplies.

When I entered recovery, I was not the only person in my family needing change. As a matter-of-fact, we all did. This is not surprising since addictive behavior is not only hereditary, it is also very contagious. But looking at the situation sober was very overwhelming. Fortunately, I did not try to take on the monumental task of fixing my family as I had been prone to do in the past. I had more than I could handle with myself.

I remember one night, shortly after leaving the treatment center, when my husband was not home, obviously out drinking as usual. This particular evening, I was struggling more than usual with the circumstances caused by his drinking and decided to go to an Al-anon meeting. This support group, which is for the families and friends of the addicted, met in a building that also housed the local AA meetings. I stood outside, undecided as to which meeting I wanted to attend. In a flash of insight I knew I had to take care of myself. If my husband was going to be taken care of and fixed, it would have to be he and God who did the work. I went through the doors of my AA meeting.

That was a very crucial moment in my life. It launched a direction in my recovery that proved to be beneficial not only to me, but to all of my family. From that time forward I was able to help pull them up from their own pits of misery instead of allowing them to pull me down with them.

Edmund Burke, a member of the British Parliament in the 1700s, said, "A nation without the means of reform is without the means of survival." I believe this, but I would go even further and say that the same is true for individuals. And what is that means of reform? God. He and He alone can affect permanent change. Ask any alcoholic, drug addict, or other addicted person how many times they attempted reformation on their own. It works for awhile, but the change is never permanent. They may never go back to practicing their actual addiction, but they are simply "dry drunks." Their lives never hold any peace and joy or true change. Only God can provide that.

Jesus answered them, verily, verily, I say unto you,
whosoever commiteth sin is the servant of sin.
John 8:34

I'm not sure what the definition of vice is, but I have a feeling it's just another of those politically correct words for sin, designed to make us feel better about our shortcomings. However, as Shakespeare said, "A rose by any other name would smell just as sweet."

I've had many vices in my lifetime. The most glaring, because it caused the most damage, was my alcoholism. Following God's divine deliverance from that addiction, others, less destructive in outward nature but just as devastating to the soul, had to be dealt with. There was smoking. What a glorious victory that was! I knew as soon as I hit the 24-hour mark without a cigarette, it was a done deal. Then there was the gambling. It's been nearly three years since I put a coin into a machine, but I find I still love the atmosphere and receive vicarious excitement through the gambling of others. I'm not sure if this is a problem, but I have a feeling that the very fact that I *don't* know means that it is. There will probably have to be further work in the future on this.

After gambling came caffeine. I had not placed too much importance on this but wanted to give it up simply because I've come to a place in my life where I don't want *anything* negative having control over me. I was pleasantly surprised when I realized I not only felt better physically but was also sleeping better as a result of eliminating it from my life.

Another major area is overeating. Unlike the others, which simply require total abstinence, overcoming an eating problem is a little more complicated, since we do have to eat. But I've got a much better handle on it than I ever have, and as my thinking continues to change, I expect continued progress.

The current area God and I are working on is impulsive overspending. Though I'm far from overcoming this, I was very excited when God first started helping me deal with it. I've had enough experience with Him and addictions to know that once He brings a problem area to my attention, it's a done deal even though outward circumstances may testify to the contrary. Another reason I'm excited about this is because I believe it to be the precursor to bountiful financial blessings He has for me. But first He has to get me to the position where He can trust me to be a good steward of those blessings. I'm not there yet, but with His continued help, I *will* get there.

Got a vice, sin, addiction, etc? Lay it at the foot of the cross. Jesus will take it up for you.

Stone #4

Lessons

*A wise man will hear, and will increase learning;
and a man of understanding shall attain unto wise
counsels...*
Proverbs 1:5

...but he for our profit (chastens us), that we might be partakers of his holiness. Now no chastening for the present seemeth to be joyous, but grievous: nevertheless afterward it yieldeth the peaceable fruit of righteousness...
Hebrews 12:10-11

I never disciplined my children. My own discipline as a child consisted of a beating with whatever was handy: belt, clothes hanger, hairbrush, etc., wielded by my mother when she was angry, which was most of the time. Because of the resentment I felt towards her form of discipline, I chose not to practice *any* form. We were both wrong, and we both raised children with a myriad of living problems resulting from our methods.

Discipline, the proper kind, is an act of love. Hebrews 12:6 says, *"For whom the Lord loveth he chasteneth..."* I sometimes say I wish He didn't love me so much. Of course, I'm only kidding, but doesn't it seem we go through periods where He doesn't let up? Those are the times I keep the above verse close to my heart because I sure want to share His holiness.

So how *does* God discipline us? I believe He works with each of us on an individual basis, depending on our personality. There are, I hear, those who greatly dislike pain and are quick to respond when it becomes evident that something in their life is not working. Which, by the way, is usually a clear signal that God is trying to move in with the discipline stick. Then there are others, and my knowledge of these is not just hearsay, who are aware their lives are not working but keep right on doing what they've always done. Their hope is that God will change their circumstances so that they themselves will not have to change.

I lived that way for 32 years as I drank my way through the prime of my life. I definitely believed in God and would frequently implore Him to change those around me, for I was sure *they* were the problem. After entering recovery, my mind cleared enough for Him to reveal the *real* problem. As Pogo, the cartoon character says,"I've met the enemy and he is us." The disciplining quickly followed this insight.

It's now been several years since I took my last drink and the program continues. The first ten years were spent learning physical discipline. Then the focus shifted to the mind and the spirit. I wish I would have been a quicker study because the rewards are incredible.

I'm finally reaching the point where God can just tap me on the shoulder and let me know something needs to be changed and I go to work on it. Oh, I may spend a day whining and feeling sorry for myself, but I no longer argue with Him for days. I've found I'm not going to change His mind so I might as well bite the bullet and jump in. It's much less painful that way and I've become one of those who really dislikes pain in my life.

The Lord will receive my prayer.
Psalm 6:9

I recently took an "Experiencing God" class. The author of the course workbook made a comment in one of the lessons that forever changed my way of thinking about prayer. He stated that he would never dream of saying a prayer without expecting an answer. That may seem pretty basic to some, but it was profoundly life changing for me.

I don't mean that prior to the course I didn't believe God answered prayer. I *knew* He did. I had seen too much proof in the lives of others as well as my own. Yes, I was definitely a believer in prayer. So where was my area of disbelief?

I suppose I thought prayer was a hit and miss operation. I figured God heard my prayers if I had been "good" the previous 24-hours (or longer if it was a really big prayer). Or if my prayer was worded exactly right. Or if I put the right amount of feeling into my prayer. Or if what I was praying was what God was going to do anyway. Mostly I prayed because God tells us to in His Word and I have a heart for obedience to Him. And He honored that desire by receiving my prayers, in spite of my screwy thinking. But I believe that through the comment in this course, God was telling me it was time for me to mature in my prayer life and develop some grown-up practices and principles.

About the same time, "coincidentally," our church's Sunday School director asked me to teach a class entitled "Discipleship Prayer Life." I hesitated, wondering how I could teach something about which God had plainly shown me I knew very little. However, I agreed, knowing that God's timing is always perfect and this class coming at this time was no accident. It has been an incredible experience and I've discovered that the best way to learn is to teach.

I wish I could say that I now have a perfect and effective prayer life, but I can't. It is better than it was, though, and like most God things, I accept that it is going to be an ongoing process that continues throughout the balance of my life.

The main thing I have learned about prayer is that God didn't order us to pray for His sake. He has everything. He doesn't need our prayers. He tells us to pray for our own benefit. Sending up our prayers makes it clear in our own minds what we want and prepares us to receive His blessings. Don't pass up this beautiful opportunity God has given to enrich your life.

For whom the Lord loveth he chasteneth...
Hebrews 12:6

My ongoing prayer is that God will keep me humble so that He won't have to make me humble. I hate humbling experiences. I can't recommend this prayer unless you're ready to get serious on God's terms because He is faithful to answer the prayer. I've just gone through one of these humbling experiences and, though it was very painful, I certainly learned something, which is, of course, the purpose behind them. Mission accomplished, God!

Every year our church has an all-day ladies retreat the last Saturday of January. Back in early November our pastor's wife, who is in charge of the retreat, asked me if I would give one of the two 45-minute presentations scheduled. I was honored and told her I would love to. That gave me nearly three full months to prepare the presentation.

The retreat is now one week away and I've not written one word. Oh, I've thought about it, occasionally prayed about it, and tossed back and forth several likely topics. Yesterday, after clearing away my other deadlines, I decided I better sit down and get the presentation on paper so I would have next week to practice it. After several starts in several different directions, I began to panic. This was most unusual for me. Nothing was coming. What I *could* get was awkward and there was no flow to anything I was writing. I started to feel the old familiar self-loathing.

I didn't sleep well last night, waking frequently with panic in my heart. I was going to give a poor performance and miss a wonderful opportunity to share my love for God with a lot of women, many of whom will be needing encouragement. I got up earlier than usual this morning, and as I sat in the early morning darkness with my cup of coffee, God revealed the problem to me.

Though I had been given plenty of time to prepare the presentation, my pride had surfaced and I treated the honor too lightly. I believed my abilities (get that—*my* abilities) would enable me to reel off the words in short order and I would give a razzle dazzle performance. Then God reminded me that without Him I can do nothing (John 15:5).

After spending some time in heartfelt sorrow, I knew I had learned the lesson He had for me and I knew that He had forgiven me. It was time to put it behind me and move forward. He then gave me the topic *He* wanted me to prepare, but even with forgiveness there are consequences. I will have to work hard and hustle to get it ready, but I know that, with God's help, it will get done and will be good. And I am a little wiser for the experience.

Is any sick among you?
James 5:14

God has blessed my husband and me with the gift of extremely good health. We are probably healthier than 90% of the people our age, in spite of the 40 years of abusive treatment we heaped upon ourselves with alcohol, smoking, inadequate diets, improper rest, and all the stress, strain, and anxiety caused by that type of living. This gift from God is something, unfortunately, I usually take for granted—until the last couple of weeks, that is.

My husband and I have both had colds, bad colds, for the last two weeks. This is only the second time in over 11 years we have been sick. I don't handle it well. It's not that I'm a whiney crybaby. Actually, I have a very high pain threshold. But when I don't feel good, I can't seem to achieve that balance for which I'm constantly striving.

As I have written elsewhere, there are certain things I have to incorporate into my days to maintain my sanity. These include exercise, prayer, Bible reading, and writing. I tried keeping up with these when I first began to get sick, but my husband insisted I stay off the stationary bicycle until I was feeling better (he doesn't insist on much, so I know I better pay attention when he does insist). So what did I do? Threw the baby out with the bath water. If I couldn't do it all, I wouldn't do any of it.

The week passed in a blur while I took care of only the basic essentials. And, surprise, surprise, my physical condition got worse. It finally dawned on me yesterday what was wrong. What God has shown me through this experience verifies something I've always believed—doing everything we can to keep our mental level high is especially important during low physical levels.

I mistakenly thought if I couldn't exercise, I just wouldn't do any of it. Even though I didn't feel like praying, reading, writing, etc., I should have forced myself to do them. That would have kept me in a proper frame of mind, thus speeding the physical healing process (once again, God uses an adverse situation to teach me a lesson).

More and more scientific and medical research is proving the link between the mind and the body. I've heard the medical profession say, "It's not important what the disease is a person has, but who the person is that has the disease." We must never underestimate the power of prayer in sickness. My husband and I realized this morning that we each prayed for our collective healing for the first time last night. Is it a coincidence that we both feel better this morning?

*And thy life shall hang in doubt before thee; and thou
shalt fear day and night, and shalt have none assurance of thy life.*
Deuteronomy 28:66

This verse is a portion of a long dissertation from God
addressed to the Israelites. He was explaining the curses
they would experience if they did not obey Him and observe
all His commandments. The list is long: confusion, rebuke,
pestilence, consumption, fever, inflammation, blight, mildew,
defeat, terror, boils, tumors, madness, blindness, and on and
on the list goes. Not a good read. But, for me where I am
today, this verse, promising dread (fear) day and night, seems
to be the worst in the list. God has very recently revealed to
me how much of my days are spent in dread.

Exactly what is dread? My dictionary says, "to be in
extreme apprehension of; to be reluctant to do, meet, or experience." It is an emotion that can suck the joy out of everyday
life. It's great to have an exciting event in our future that we
can look forward to with anticipation, such as a long awaited
vacation, a birthday party, or a visit from the kids. We love
the grand things of life. But the truth is, these are but a small
portion of our time. The majority of our reality is spent in the
everyday Monday, Tuesday, Wednesday living. If we don't
derive our joy and peace from these ordinary routine times,
we are missing some of God's greatest blessings.

God has shown me that I was getting my joy from what
I look forward to in the future, like a trip to town for dinner
and a movie, a camping vacation, etc. I have not been living
in the moment. My everyday moments are spent in dread,
starting with my eyes opening in the morning dreading to
get up. I dread having to exercise, fix my face and hair, pray
(forgive me, God), write, work, laundry, cleaning, washing
the car, bathing the dog, watering the plants, studying, and
all of life's other mundane tasks. And yet, these things are

what, when combined, make up the very fabric of my life. They are who I am—what I do with the majority of my time. Thank God I've gotten past the point of deciding whether or not I'm going to do them. I know I am going to complete all of these things, and yet I still dread them. It's crazy!

As always, I know my solution is God. I'm unable to change without His help, as I've proven countless times in the past. Evidently, the time is right to work on this since it was Him who brought it to my attention. I don't know exactly what the process will be, but if I stay close, He will guide me through it—of that I can be certain.

*For my thoughts are not your thoughts, neither are
your ways my ways, saith the Lord. For as the heavens
are higher than the earth, so are my ways higher than
your ways, and my thoughts than your thoughts.*
Isaiah 55:8-9

I constantly pray that God will not allow me to limit Him
to my small ways and my small thinking. My goal is to arrive
at the place where I can say to Him, "Here's the problem,
God. You already know about it and I trust You to handle it
as You see fit, knowing that You see the big picture and my
scope seldom goes beyond my little corner of the world." I
haven't totally accomplished this yet. I still want to get in
there and say, "Now God, here's the problem and this is the
way I think You should solve it."

It's getting easier, though, for me to just turn it over to
Him. The reason it is easier is because of a couple of situations I faced and had no advice to give Him as to possible
solutions. And, of course, since I couldn't see an answer,
I was sure He would not be able to do anything with the
problem. Imagine my surprise when He not only came up
with solutions, but did it much faster without my help!

I've found that usually even when I "say" I've totally
given Him a problem, I still keep my hands on it. In the
back of my mind I have the best possible solution worked
out and that is where I keep my eyes, instead of on Him;
that is where I direct my efforts, instead of listening for His
direction. This is a common mistake many of us make. It's
also a sad mistake. Because of our preconceived notions of
what is the best way for our lives to be lived, we limit God.
I will give you an example of what I mean. Recently our
cash flow simply wasn't flowing. After writing checks for
the monthly bills, I found I was going to be short $847 in the
household account.

God has been dealing with me for several months about becoming a better steward with *all* that He gives, but particularly in the area of finances. I was watching my spending and depending on Him to supply our needs, which you can do when you're operating in the realm of obedience. I told Him about coming up $847 short (as if He didn't already know), and pretty much left it to Him. But in the back of my mind I figured the best way for Him to bring the needed money was in the form of a new subscription for my monthly publication. Based on *my* thoughts, I was watching the mail for the order. A few days later, my husband comes home with a $3000 Christmas bonus. He had never received a Christmas bonus in the nine years he had worked for the company. God came through the back door, and, fortunately, it turned out all right even though I had limited Him to my small ways and small thoughts. I let it serve as a reminder to me that if I will leave things to Him, they could turn out much better than I could ever plan or even imagine.

...let us run with patience the race that is set before
us looking unto Jesus the author and finisher of our
faith...
Hebrews 12:1-2

Several years ago I had a drawing that I kept on the refrigerator. Apparently it's been lost in a move somewhere along the way, but I still think of it often and am always on the lookout for another one like it. It was a picture of Daniel in the lion's den. He is standing, hands folded behind him, head lifted towards heaven with a peaceful, serene look on his face. The lions are a respectable distance behind him, simply staring at him. There was no caption with the picture, but none was needed. The message was clear: no matter what the circumstances, keep your eyes on God.

God doesn't promise us a smooth life without adversity. As a matter-of-fact, the opposite is true. He says that in this world we *will* have tribulations, but then He immediately tells us to cheer up for He has overcome the world (John 16:33). So while we are assured of problems, He also gives us the solution. We are to cheer up and, as the above verse tells us, *"run with patience the race before us,"* which I see as life in general, and most importantly, we are to keep our eyes on Jesus.

Circumstances come and go. If we live our lives based on what we see, the ever-changing situations that weave their way throughout our days, we will never accomplish any measure of stability. We must take things as they come, deal with them, and keep our eyes on Jesus, trusting that He will cause even the seemingly "bad" things in our lives to come together for the good as He promises in Romans 8:28.

I've developed a pretty simple method of determining if I've taken my eyes off Jesus. If I've lost my joy or if frustration has set in, I know I'm looking at circumstances and need to lift my eyes. I believe others could also use this as a gauge. For example, my husband is the most even-keeled person I've ever known (one of his traits for which I am most grateful). Yet this week, he has not quite been himself. It's nothing that anyone else would probably even notice, but it bothered me because I knew something was wrong. I finally asked him last night and he admitted he is frustrated over the lack of progress of putting a new engine in his truck. There have been obstacles and unforseen delays, just like in life. He's got his eyes on the circumstances. Perhaps he will be able to lift them back to Jesus, who also has an interest in his truck.

The formula is simple, be patient and focus on Jesus. All we have to do is follow it.

...she shall be called woman...
Genesis 2:23

The gentleman who wrote <u>Men are from Mars and Women are from Venus</u> had a rare insight into the differences between the sexes. He has done much for relationships in the world and my hat is off to him for sharing his knowledge.

Women are very special creatures, God's finest creation. There is a joke that goes like this, "God made man, looked at him, decided he could do better, so He made woman." It's funny, but I believe there might be a note of truth to it and I believe there are a lot of men who will agree with me.

I think the women's lib movement is the most tragic move women ever made. In my opinion, any attempt to put us on an equal level with men brings us down, not raises us. We fought for free sex. Well, we got it and now our 9 and 10-year-old daughters are getting pregnant and sexually transmitted diseases are at epidemic proportions. The sanctity of marriage is a joke and lasting relationships are nearly a thing of the past.

We fought for equality in the work place and we got it too. Now we can boast the same (if not higher) rate of heart attacks as men. And thanks to being free to pursue a career, statistics say nearly 75% of the country's children return home from school each day to an empty house. Mom stops by the fast food joint on the way home, lets the kids grab a paper plate and fills it full of high fat, low nutrition, junk food. She's either much too tired to ask or even care about their day, or she brought work home and hasn't the time to mess with them. This is the same mother that will ask, "Where did I go wrong?" when her kids become involved in undesirable behavior.

It's tragic what we are doing to our children, but what we have done to our men is equally sad. God created man to protect his family and to go out and work to provide for that family. We have taken that responsibility from him by going out to earn our own living and expecting him to take over half of our God-given responsibilities. He is confused and frightened because he doesn't know what is expected of him, and he doesn't know how to perform the new duties we have forced on him.

The women's movement has destroyed the traditional family unit and everyone is paying the high cost including the women.

If I had not come and spoken unto them, they had not
sin, but now they have no cloak for their sin.
John 15:22

This morning I woke with a guilt-laden conscience. I hate it when that happens! Several months ago as I was watering my houseplants, I over-watered one. Unfortunately, it was the one I had sitting on top of the satellite receiver connected to the television (lesson number 1: don't put plants on top of the little black boxes). The insides fried as soon as the water touched them. Expensive lesson there was a $100 replacement cost.

It doesn't take me long to learn. I sure didn't put the plant on top of the new receiver, I put it beside it instead. This is an airplane plant and the leaves can act as funnels when the water hits them. Yes, you guessed it. A few evenings ago my husband was helping me water (thank goodness it was him this time) and several drops of water ran down a leaf that was hanging over the receiver (lesson number 2: don't put a plant anywhere near the little black box).

My immediate reaction was, "Oh no, another $100!" The following day I called the satellite company and then the manufacturer to see if maybe, just maybe, it wasn't ruined. I didn't lie to them. I simply didn't tell them what had happened. They walked me through several steps and, of course, nothing worked. No problem. It was still under warranty. They would send out a technician to either repair or replace it.

My conscience kicked in and I started the routine. You know the one. The cloaks. "We just paid $100 for this five months ago. Maybe it wasn't the water. Maybe it's just a coincidence that it went out at the same time as the water got on it. We're talking a big company here. They can afford it. Everyone does it." And it almost worked. Until God hit me this morning before I was awake enough to have my defenses in place (sometimes He doesn't play fair).

There was nothing complex to analyze or discuss. The question was simple. Do I have values or don't I? Values are useless if I profess them when it's easy, convenient, and they don't cost me anything, but toss them to the winds when things get a little difficult or costly. In a few seconds God revealed to me how this type of little compromise will eat away at a person's integrity. Eventually loss of integrity infects the family unit, the community, the state, and ultimately the nation. Think that's being a bit melodramatic over such a small thing? Just look around you at the state of your nation.

Oh yes, about the satellite receiver, we bought a new one.

Stone #5

Answers

And all that heard him were astonished at his under-standing and answers.
Luke 2:47

Give therefore thy servant an understanding heart that
I may discern between good and bad.
1 Kings 3:9

What an incredible discovery it was for me to realize first what discernment actually is, and then that I could pray for it and God would give it to me.

My first prayer for discernment came about as a result of being sick and tired of living in that dark place of constant guilt. All my life I had felt guilty. Now granted, some of it was legitimate (actually, a lot of it), but much of it was not. I would feel guilty when those around me were not happy, even though intellectually I knew I could not possibly be the source of their unhappiness. I carried the weight of the world on my shoulders.

After being in recovery ten years, growing in my walk with God, and with His help, ridding my life of much of the ugly stuff, I realized the guilt never lifted. Common sense told me that with all the good God had brought into my life, I should be experiencing at least *some* guilt-free moments. That's when I began to take a close look at the guilt and realized Satan was really doing a number on me, and I had been allowing it all my life. Right here I had two choices (this was one of those moments of decision). I could continue living under the heavy cloud of condemnation, thus rendering an effective witness for God almost impossible, or I could go to God and ask for His help. I chose the latter. As I prayed for God to show me a better way to live, I was led by the Spirit to pray for discernment between God's conviction of my sins and Satan's condemnation. That prayer was rewarded with an answer almost immediately.

I began to realize that when Satan condemns me, he does it for one reason only: to make me feel bad about myself, which makes me useless to God. God's conviction, on the other hand, is a gentle (gentle in the beginning, anyway) awareness of a problem area in my life such as a wrong thought, a bad attitude, or an ungodly deed. It is *always* a call to action, a call to change something. If I am immediately obedient, coming into agreement with Him, asking for and accepting His forgiveness, seeking His help in the change, and committing to it, there is no bad feeling and no self-loathing. Only an incredible feeling of being loved and watched over.

Since that time, there have been other areas in which I have prayed for divine discernment and He is faithful to grant it. I believe, however, that we must always be willing to go in whatever direction that discernment indicates. He is not going to supply it just for our amusement.

God is not the author of confusion, but of peace...
1 Corinthians 14:33

When Paul wrote these words to the Corinthians he was addressing the confusion that was taking place in the church service but I believe we can use his message in other circumstances today. God is *not* the author of confusion, and I am learning to use that fact as a yardstick in my own life. If I am in the midst of a confusing situation or my mind is on that awful treadmill, going around and around a problem or a decision for which there seems to be no solution, well, it's time to back off and re-evaluate.

I am presently in the middle of just such a situation. As I have mentioned elsewhere, I write a monthly publication for prison inmates. I absolutely know that God called me to that particular ministry. But I've also learned that just because He calls a person to something, doesn't mean it's a forever thing. Some things are only for a season. Now, I understand there are some people who give up too easily. They turn tail and run at the very first obstacle. I'm not one of those people. No, I will beat a dead horse and hang in there long after God is through with something. He practically has to pry things from my fingers when it's time to let go and move on to the next thing.

Here's my dilemma. My publication has not accomplished wild success by the world's standards. That was never one of my criteria for doing it, though I have to admit it sure would be nice. I'm now in my fifth year having just sent out my 50th issue. The main theme of the whole publication is change; admitting it is needed and how to obtain it. It's getting increasingly more difficult to come up with different ways to say the same thing.

Is God trying to tell me He's finished with it and it's time for me to move on? Or do I just want to back out because *I'm* ready for something new and because my ingenuity is being challenged? I honestly don't know hence the confusion. I know myself well enough to not trust my own motives, and I want to be as certain as possible before I make a move on this. It's far too important of a decision to make hastily. God is not a God of confusion, so one thing I can be certain of is that my confusion is not coming from Him.

But the fruit of the Spirit is love, joy, peace, long-
suffering, gentleness, goodness, faith, meekness,
temperance...
Galations 5:23

1 Corinthians 6:19 tells me that the Holy Spirit lives in me; my body is His temple. This is true of all believers. My Bible dictionary tells me that fruit means "produce, crop, harvest." Taking the verse and the definition and putting them together, I conclude that I should be full to overflowing with the attributes listed in the Galations verse. So why am I not?

If I am honest (which I try always to be), I have to say humbly that I do often display all these fruits (though seldom at the same time). But I acknowledge that it comes straight from the Holy Spirit because I certainly haven't always been that way. However, if the Holy Spirit is living in me, these qualities should be a regular part of my life, not just a smile and a show of patience in the grocery store line after church. I don't want it to be a "hit and miss" thing in my life. I want these evidences of the Holy Spirit to pervade every nook, cranny, and corner of my being. I want them to be as much a part of me as breathing. I want people to look at me and see Jesus.

You're probably saying to yourself, "Well, she doesn't want much, does she?" I don't think it is too much to ask. After all, God Himself has told me in His word that it is all available to me through the Holy Spirit with whom my mind, heart, and soul share this body. Why would God provide the abundance and give me a burning desire to possess it if it were out of the realm of possibility? I don't believe He would. So no, I'm not asking too much. But how do I make these beautiful fruits a part of my very being?

Before I answer this question (like I really have an answer), I just noticed something. The verse says these qualities are the fruit of the Spirit, not the fruits of the Spirit. It seems to me like it's one package. I believe we make a mistake when we look at these as individual goals on which to work. For instance, I might wake up tomorrow morning and say, "I feel pretty good. I think I'll work on the fruit of love today." Or, "I feel like yelling at everyone this morning, I guess it would be a good day to work on peace and patience." These kinds of thoughts and endeavors take our attention away from the main issue and place it on our works (Satan just loves it when that happens).

Our primary focus here is to be the Holy Spirit. If we allow Him to permeate our every thought, word, and action, the fruit outlined in this verse is going to be a natural manifestation. God is not interested in our works or what we do to better ourselves. He is interested in us allowing His Holy Spirit to work within us to bring us ever closer to the image of His Son.

*And ye shall seek me, and find me, when ye shall
search for me with all your heart.*
Jeremiah 29:13

My husband and I live in a small town about 115 miles
north of Las Vegas. When I say small, I don't mean just in
comparison to Las Vegas—I mean small in comparison to
anything. We have three casinos, two service station/mini
marts, several bars, and one post office. I learned early not to
run out of bread on Sunday because the bread truck doesn't
come until Tuesday.

I don't really mind living here because I'm not a shopper
(though a real grocery store *would* be nice), we are not
particularly social people, and our days of enjoying the
nightlife are long past. But I have to admit, there have been
times when I've questioned God about why we are here. One
reason I know we're here, which I'm very grateful for, is my
husband's very good job. It's going a long way in providing
the means for a comfortable retirement. It was definitely an
answer to a prayer that we sent up when we first came to this
area years ago.

My "why" questions have centered more on what God
has for me personally in this remote area. I want to work for
Him so much. I did volunteer to do weekly basic life skills
presentations at a homeless shelter in Las Vegas and to a
group of ex-inmates. I loved it and did it for over a year, but
then I had to look at it realistically. It was taking two days
a week of my time (one for preparation, one for travel and
presentation). It was expensive with the cost of gas and wear
and tear on the car. And my husband constantly worried
about me being on the road so late at night as the presentations were in a less than desirable section of town.

Then there is our church. It is in a town 75 miles away. I
love the church and the people and would be there every time

the doors open if I could. But once again, time and expense allow for only a couple of times a week.

I believe I have recently received some insight into the reasons for my isolation. Because of my very nature, I have the tendency to get out of balance in everything I do, so perhaps He has me in a place where distractions are not an issue. Though volunteer and church work, and worship and fellowship are all good and important, He wants me to search for *Him* with all my heart. Not easy to do. It's much easier to get out and "do something" so I can feel good about myself. And it is true that faith without words is dead, but I need first to search for God with all my heart and then *He* will lead me to the works He desires for me.

*In the morning, O LORD, you hear my voice; in the
morning I lay my requests before you and wait in
expectation.*
Psalm 5:3

I've prayed all my life, at least as far back as I can
remember. But not until recently have I begun to understand
and believe in the power of prayer. Oh, I've always believed
God answers prayer, but I figured the answered ones were
for other people — not for me.

I was always sure there was a formula and secret key to
getting prayers answered and I was certain that "right" living
was a part of it. I didn't live right and I wasn't good enough
for God to even listen to my prayers, much less answer them.
So why would a person who felt that way continue to pray? I
have no satisfactory answer. I knew I was "supposed" to and
that His Word instructs us to. Perhaps I thought the law of
averages would kick in and I was bound to get an occasional
answer. Maybe I was afraid not to. Or I could have thought
that if I kept at it, I could stumble on that magic formula. I
don't know the reason. I just know I kept praying.

I now know God was hearing all those prayers I offered
up. He didn't answer them as I wished (thank goodness),
but His answers were what I needed (regardless of what I
thought at the time). And I hadn't been totally wrong. There
is a secret key to prayer. It's revealed where all His other
secrets are — in His Word. First I must believe that He is the
rewarder of those who diligently seek Him (Hebrews 11:6).
Then I must pray according to His will (1 John 5:14-15).
How do I know what His will is? By reading His Word.

I will be the first to admit that I can't always find chapter
and verse for those things about which I need to pray. But
there are guidelines. Suppose I want to buy a new car but
don't know if it's the right thing to do. There's not one verse
in the Bible that addresses new cars. But there are verses

about checking our motives and there are verses about being a good steward. Knowing God's will for our lives is not as difficult as we sometimes make it out to be.

When we are seeking God's will for our lives, as the above verse says, we can order our prayers to God and then wait in expectation for the answers. I recently took an "Experiencing God" course and the author of the workbook said that he would never dream of uttering a prayer without expecting an answer. That may seem like a given to some, but it was a profound revelation to me that has changed my whole prayer life. With incredibly positive results, I might add.

To make the weight for the winds; and he weigheth the
water by measure. When he made a decree for the rain,
and way for the lightning of the thunder...
Job 28:25-26

One of my recent daily devotionals suggested, "Thank God for teaching you to have limits." These eight simple words hit me right in the middle of my being. I realized in a flash of insight straight from God that limits are at the very foundation of most of my problems. I don't have any limits. Well, that's not quite true. Everyone has limits. I just don't acknowledge mine.

As far back as I can remember, I've done everything to excess: drinking, working, eating, etc. My husband dreads to see vacations end because I never want them to and I sink into a quiet depression on the way home. I eat until I'm miserable. And I drank the same way. If I couldn't sit down and get sloshy drunk, I wouldn't even have a drink. I never understood those people who could have one drink and then walk away. I remember (and I use that word loosely) my husband and I going into a bar one morning at 8:00 and not leaving until closing time which was 2:00 the next morning, and leaving upset because it was closing time.

Why is this? I seldom enjoy the activity in which I'm currently engaged. No, I'm too busy dreading the impending end of it. I believe, however, that God is working with me to correct this most paralyzing defect. That is the reason the sentence in the devotional caught my mind and my heart. I have a feeling the defect is not going to go easily.

The above verse tells me that God sets limits on everything: the winds, the waters, the rain, the thunder. And that means there are limits in our personal lives, or at least, there should be.

Limits explain why I'm having a problem bringing some seemingly minor problems under control while the major ones went all at once. With my drinking, smoking, and gambling, total abstinence was the simple solution (simple does not necessarily equate to easy). However, eating is another matter. I *have* to eat, and one bite can invoke an eating frenzy. No limits.

So what's the answer here? As with everything, the answer lies with God. I know nothing about setting limits and staying within them. I must look to Him to teach me and then to operate within them on a consistent (there's that awful word again) basis. I know from past experiences that God's timing is perfect, so I am ready for this new challenge regardless of what my feelings tell me.

...and bring into captivity every thought to the obedience of Christ.
Corinthians 10:5

Taking every thought captive? This sounds like warfare to me, and it is.

They say that the average person has 60,000 thoughts a day ("they" being the people who count such things. I've always secretly wondered about "them" too). 60,000 thoughts a day. Now granted, there may be some, like the junkie looking for his next fix or the mother with four children under the age of six, who have the same thought 60,000 times a day. But for the majority of us, there are a variety of thoughts racing in and out.

How does a person even begin the monumental task of bringing 60,000 thoughts into captivity for Christ? Well, I can tell you right now that without Christ, it's impossible. So before you even start, and I assume you are going to start since this verse calls us to do it, drop to your knees and tell God you want to be obedient but it is too great an undertaking for you to attempt without His help.

The first thing (after the prayer) called for here is to become aware of the thoughts that normally march undetected through our minds. Once you start monitoring them, you're going to be surprised at the useless, unproductive, and sometimes downright sleazy quality of your thinking. While this may be a shock, don't let it discourage you or produce undue guilt.

We have no control over what enters our minds. But once something has come in, we do have control over what we do with it. If it's an undesirable negative thought, we face a choice. We can either sit down and fellowship with it, entertaining it in such a way that it expands and takes over, or we can immediately dismiss it and replace it with a positive godly thought.

Speaking of which, I would like to qualify my statement that we have no control over what enters our minds. We're always going to have that occasional dark unbidden thought that causes us to wonder where in the world it originated. But to a great extent, we do have control over our thoughts. One of God's great laws of the universe is "like attracts like." If we fill our minds with positives through Bible reading, prayer, fellowship with other believers, good motivational tapes and books, etc., it just follows that most of our thoughts are going to center around these things.

God will help you in this process. He will alert you to the thinking He wants out of your life and then together you will take it captive one thought at a time.

If my people which are called by My name, shall
humble themselves and pray and seek My face, and
turn from their wicked ways; then will I hear from
heaven, and will forgive their sin, and will heal their
land.
2 Chronicles 7:14

There has been another school shooting this week. Kids killing kids. The real tragedy is that it was only news for a couple of days, being overridden by an erratic stock market. The killings among our children are becoming so common we've become apathetic (just as the Bible warns will happen in the last days).

Yesterday I heard of a young boy who killed his sister while imitating the wrestling he sees on television. When this type of tragedy occurs, many say, "What's wrong with these kids?" Or, "The parents should be more careful about what the children watch on TV."

We want to point fingers and pass the blame. The school killings have set the anti-gun supporters into a frenzy. Make stiffer laws. Take the guns away. Can't these people see that the guns are not the problem? Guns have been around for a long time. When I was in high school nearly every teenage boy had a gun on a rack behind the front seat of his truck that he used for hunting. Most households had at least one gun and the kids were not killing each other with them. No, the answer is not more laws.

The above verse tells us very plainly what the answer is. We must humble ourselves and pray and seek God's ways, and turn from our own evil ways. Humbling ourselves means to admit we were wrong, that perhaps we don't know everything after all. Maybe rock and roll should have been banned back in the 50's. Maybe taking prayer and the Ten Commandments out of the schools wasn't such a good idea. Maybe the women's lib movement took things too far in their quest for equal rights and sexual freedom. Humbling is painful, but it's necessary for true change to begin.

The rest of the "ifs" are self-explanatory. We must pray. About what? Everything. We must seek God. How is that done? By getting into His word. Malachi 3:6 tells us, *"For I am the Lord, I change not. "* Therefore, everything we need to know about Him is in His word, nothing has changed. He is the same today as He was when the words were written. And finally, as I said, we must turn from our wicked ways.

Every morning that the sun rises tells me that God is not yet through with man—that there is still hope. But the predicted signs of the end (including kids killing kids) are all around us. I don't know how much longer He will tarry. Each of us has a responsibility to obey the above verse and begin to turn our country back towards God so that He will hear us, forgive our sin, and heal our land.

...said I not unto thee, that, if thou wouldest believe;
thou shouldest see the glory of God?
John 11:40

God, forgive me for my unbelief. I returned last night from a two-day faith conference that was undoubtedly the most incredible spiritual experience of my life. There were thirteen ladies from our church that attended the conference and we definitely saw the Glory of God in all its magnificent splendor.

Two of the ladies from the group and I agreed to pray all week preceding the conference for a personal miracle for each of the thirteen. We didn't pray for specific miracles, though some have very obvious needs, but just for God to look into each of our lives and provide us with the miracle He wanted to bestow, knowing that He is more cognizant of our needs than we are. I can't speak for the others. I don't know if each one received her miracle or not. If not, I believe it's because she failed to recognize it, for I am convinced that God answered our prayers and provided the miracle; a personalized, customized miracle for each of us. I will tell you what He did for me.

I have been in a real life slump for about the last month. It has been more than the usual "valley walking" time that most people (yes, even we Christians) occasionally experience. It has actually bordered on a full-blown depression, which I have not experienced in many years. It was triggered by a simple move from one house to another. Simple yes, but not easy, and it brought home to me, in what I thought was a pretty cruel manner, the fact that I no longer have the physical capabilities of the young. In other words, I came face to face with the reality of my age, and though I am a professed positive thinker, I just could not seem to come to grips with this truth. Until the conference and my miracle, that is.

It just so happened (yeah, right) that all the women speakers, with a couple of exceptions, are at least 65 years old and some are even a few pounds overweight. They are dynamic, energetic, and funny. They are not "Ms. Super Christian", but are simply women with flaws (which none had tried to erase with face lifts), who have experienced the same problems as all of us. They have the same doubts and fears that weave in and out of my life and they are not afraid to express them and to laugh about them, and yes, even to cry about them.

God showed me in a most remarkable way that my life is far from over. Yes, I am entering a different season and some adjustments have to be made, but with God it can be the best and most exciting season yet. Thank You, God, for my miracle.

For that which I do I allow not: for what I would, that
do I not, but what I hate, that do I.
Romans 7:15

The above verse, and those that follow through verse 25, were written by Paul approximately 25-years after his conversion, so we're not talking about a brand new Christian who was having trouble sorting things out and resisting temptation. No, we're talking about a seasoned man of God who had been spreading the good news of the Gospel for years.

I awoke about 4:00 this morning with waves of guilt and condemnation washing over me (Satan always attacks when we're at our most vulnerable). I haven't just strayed from my eating plan; I've abandoned it as though I had been on a 40-day fast and was in danger of starving to death if I didn't eat everything in sight. Why is this?

Just like Paul in the above verse, I don't understand. I don't want to overeat. Besides the mental anguish it causes, I'm quickly undoing the progress I made with my weight. What's really strange when this happens is the fact that I don't just eat a few things I shouldn't—I eat past the point of being miserable and then continue on. It's the addiction thing. I eat the same way I used to drink. So what's the solution?

If I knew the answer to that I wouldn't be writing on the subject today. However, I do know a couple of things that are not the solution and for me that's often where I have to start.

One non-solution is wallowing in self-pity and guilt. Satan would like for me to believe that I cannot keep going to God over and over with the same sin. As is typical of his attacks, there is a grain of truth to this (if he told us out and out lies we would pay no attention to him). I can't go to God over and over with the same sin unless there is true repentance in the heart and a sincere desire and intention to turn away from the sin. Remember that God looks at the heart.

I have that intention and that desire. I am determined. No matter how many times I slip and fall, I'm going to continue to get up and start again with God's help. Guilt and condemnation renders us unproductive and ineffective, which is, of course, the reason Satan tries to keep us operating within that heavy realm. Thank God I am learning I don't have to give in to his tactics.

Guilty? Yes, I am. Consequences? Yes, there are. But I accept both and allow God to wash away the guilt and help me deal with the consequences.

*Beware when all that thou hast is multiplied, then thy
heart be lifted up and thou forget the Lord thy God...*
Deuteronomy 8:11,13-14

These verses seem innocent enough at first glance, but
they are a stern warning from God that needs to be heeded.
The words were spoken to the Israelites as they were about
to enter the Promised Land after their 40-year trek through
the wilderness. There would be obstacles to overcome but
God knew there would also be many luxuries they would
enjoy for which they would not have to work. He knew this
to be a dangerous situation; and hence the warning.

The United States is currently the most prosperous
country in the world. We are also the envy of the world, the
most sought after destination of immigrants and vacationers.
And we have failed to heed the warning God gave to the
Israelites. We've forgotten our Lord who brought us into the
land of plenty. And we are paying the cost.

We allowed prayer to be taken out of the schools and
now the children are killing each other. In this #1 country in
the world, we have a 25% illiteracy rate among adults. We
turned our heads as a past president, the highest elected official in the country, flaunted his adulterous affair in our face,
the affair that was taking place in the White House which we
support with our tax dollars. Then we listened to and allowed
him to lie to us on national television. We overlooked his
sins because the economy was good and we didn't want to
rock the boat.

Parents feel they must make a name for themselves in
their profession and climb that corporate ladder of success.
Never mind if they have to step on a few heads on the way
up and make unethical compromises along the way. That's
just how the game is played. They never give a thought to
the fact that their children are coming home to an empty
house every day. Sacrifices have to be made by every family

member if they are to have his and hers BMWs, the super sound system with DVD player, the 60" high definition television, the swimming pool with Jacuzzi and sauna. After all, the kids are enjoying these "things" too.

Where's God in all this? Like I said, we haven't heeded His warning. We've forgotten that this great country was built on godly principles. We've forgotten God. And I fear that, unless there is a change, true to His Biblical pattern, He is going to turn us over to our own heart's lusts (Psalm 81:12); give us enough rope to hang ourselves. The solution? Just as we see the cause of the problem in the Bible, we can also find our answer. 2 Chronicles 7:14, *"and if my people which are called by my name, shall humble themselves, and pray, and seek my face, and turn from their wicked ways, then will I hear from heaven, and will forgive their sin, and will heal their land."*

He that getteth riches, and not by right, shall leave them in the midst of his days, and at his end shall be a fool.
Jeremiah 17:11

Everywhere you turn today, someone is shouting about, "My rights my rights. What about my rights!" The sad part about this situation is that, quite often, those who shout the loudest have the least right to the rights they are demanding.

I don't think our founding fathers had any idea the nightmare their Bill of Rights would create several centuries later. Their ideas were good, their intentions purposeful. However, there was no way they could foresee a generation that would demand their rights but refuse to accept their responsibilities. Thomas Paine, American political theorist and writer, said, "Those who expect to reap the blessings of freedom must, like men, undergo the fatigue of supporting it." Noble thought and an absolute truth, in theory. Too bad it isn't in practice today.

We have people incarcerated for committing crimes against society and the government who are actually suing that very government (and in many cases winning) because their "rights" were violated. I was under the impression that all but the basic rights (to be treated in a humane manner) were relinquished when the guilty verdict is passed. Don't get me wrong, I'm all for rehabilitation. I work hard in my professional life and as a volunteer in my private life to help prisoners turn their lives around. But I believe the way to do this is to help them accept their fair share of responsibility, not to encourage them to blame their problems on others by giving merit to their frivolous lawsuits.

Schools can no longer correct the students. Parents can't discipline their children. Employers cannot correct their employees. Who is responsible for this? The government, the system. As is their usual way, what started out as a good idea was allowed to get out of hand. Ridiculous lawsuits are given serious time, consideration, and money. When one of our grandsons was 10 years old, he got a blister on his foot from his new tennis shoes and said he should consider suing the manufacturer. A thought like this would never cross the mind of a 10-year-old unless he had been brought up in a society who sues at the drop of a hat and a system that allows it.

Where is the self-responsibility? Whatever happened to, "Gee, those shoes are a little tight. I probably shouldn't have worn them all day.?" Rights? Yes, we have a lot of them, but each one comes with a responsibility.

*And the Lord said unto Cain, Why art thou wroth? And
why is thy countenance fallen? If thou doest well, shalt
thou not be accepted? And if thou doest not well, sin
lieth at the door. And unto thee shall be his desire, and
thou shalt rule over him.*
Genesis 4:6-7

The main message I get from this verse is that if I do
well, everything is going to be okay within me. Maybe not
on the outside. Maybe not in my circumstances. But within.
And after all, within is where our reality is anyway.

Leading up to this verse, Cain and his brother, Abel, were
bringing sacrifices to the Lord. God was pleased with Abel's
sacrifice but not with Cain's. Cain became angry and God
admonished him with the above verse. Cain eventually killed
his brother out of jealousy and then wandered the land alone
without God. Sad story. Cain didn't change God's mind with
his anger. He only made things worse for himself.

I have found that when I get really angry, which, thank
God, is very seldom, it's because I have done something
wrong and it's been called to my attention by someone else.
Unfortunately for him, it's usually my husband. I'm not
talking righteous anger over a legitimate injustice against
me. Generally my anger is simply a defense so I won't have
to admit my own wrong. Just as Cain's anger was.

God told Cain what the problem was, then He gave Him
the solution. God is like that. I used to dread the next ugly
He was going to expose in my life. Each one would bring
condemnation to my soul and I would go around for days
feeling bad about myself. Then I began to realize that was
not the reason God confronted me with them. He does it
because He loves me and my uglies block me from living
the life of joy and blessings He has for me.

I can't say I squeal with excitement when a new one
comes to my attention, but I do welcome God's revelation of

each ugly. I know He is right there to help me, and each one I put behind me brings me closer to Him.

The solution God gave Cain is the same solution He gives us thousands of years later. Doing well will change our countenance. All we have to do is well. And if we don't? Just as with Cain, so with us.

Sin truly is crouching at the door waiting for us. Ephesians 4:27 tell us, *"Neither give place to the devil."* How do we give place to him? According to the above verse, by not doing well. But it doesn't have to be that way. God tells us me must master sin and He's right there to help us do just that.

> *...and ye shall know the truth, and the truth shall make*
> *you free.*
> John 8:32

This statement by Jesus interests me greatly at this particular time because I'm desperately seeking freedom from the bondage of overeating. And it is bondage as real as any physical shackles. I felt, just a few short months ago, that I had finally conquered the problem. I was sure my victory was secure and that I was forever free from Satan's lures in that area. Read these previous three sentences and you will see one of the problems: "I felt—I had—I was." Job 12:19 tells us that God overthrows the mighty ones and Proverbs 16:18 is pretty plain, "Pride goeth before destruction, and a haughty spirit before a fall." There was definitely a haughty spirit, *No problem, I've got this under control now.* I had even reached the point of judging others in this area. *You could lose that weight if you just had the discipline I have.* Very dangerous territory on which to tread. I see that now.

Immensely humbled, I go back and start again, hopefully much wiser. I have to admit I've been very tempted to accept my weight where it is. After all, we're only talking 10 or 15 pounds and that's not so bad. There are those out there with a much bigger (literally) problem. (Recognize Satan's voice?) But I know that I know that I know if I buy into that, this time next year I'll be writing the same thing only the 10 or 15 pounds will have become 20 or 25 pounds.

To help me find the answer, I've been listening to a tape about controlling overeating. The author suggests we may need to ask God to reveal to us the reasons we overeat. I've always said I simply have an addictive personality. God has me reconsidering that statement. I don't think He's going to allow me to use that as an excuse for my undisciplined behavior any longer. It's true, I have been challenged with many addictions, but perhaps it's time to look for the real reason instead of blaming it on my genes. Therefore, I am asking God, if it will serve a positive purpose in my pursuit of freedom from the slavery of my behaviors, to reveal the reason(s) to me. And with the revelation, I pray for the courage to allow Him to heal them. If this proves to be something He lets me know that could be beneficial to others, I will share the journey with you.

*..their throat is an open sepulchre; they flatter with
their tongue.*
Psalm 5:9

There is a distinct difference between praise and flattery. The following are my own definitions (excuse me Mr. Webster). Praise is complementing someone for something they have done truly well. It is sincere, honest, and comes from the heart. Flattery, on the other hand, is an insincere complement given in the hope of getting something beneficial in return, or, in other words, sucking up. Don't ever engage in flattery. Any rewards you receive will be short-lived and will earn you the reputation of being shallow and your word will become worthless.

Praise, however, is a whole other story. It should be given lavishly, often, and to many. John Masefield, English poet, said, "Once in a century a man may be ruined or made insufferable by praise. But surely once a minute someone generous dies for want of it." So maybe it does backfire once in a century, but don't withhold something so valuable based on those kinds of odds.

It is my opinion that if we would praise our children at least as often as we criticize them, I'm merely suggesting equal time here, our country would not be experiencing the problems we now have with our youth. Constant criticism that is never balanced out with praise results in low self-esteem, which results in an unbelievable myriad of personality and behavior problems. But you don't have to believe me. Just go spend an afternoon talking to prisoners about their childhood.

I once read of an inmate who was overheard saying, "I'm so glad I didn't disappoint my dad. He always said I would end up in prison and here I am." Most prisoners will tell you that all through childhood they were told they were worthless and would never amount to anything. There are exceptions, of course, but the vast majority never received praise in their formative years.

Why are people reluctant to give praise when it is obviously due? I don't pretend to have an answer, but I do have a theory. People seem to have the idea that there is only so much glory, recognition, and credit to go around (an idea implanted by our competitive, gold, silver, bronze, loser mentality). Consequently, the feeling is, "If I tell you what a good job you did, that's less points for me," which is ridiculous. That's like saying there's just so much love to go around (another popular misconception).

Resist the temptation to flatter, but try praising others generously. You will never be sorry.

Stone #6

God's Word

*And Jesus answered him, saying, It is written, That
man shall not live by bread alone, but by every word
of God.*
Luke 4:4

All scripture is given by inspiration of God, and is profitable for doctrine, for reproof, for correction, for instruction in righteousness: that the man of God may be perfect, throughly furnished unto all good works.
2 Timothy 3:16-17

What a miracle God's Word is. Take a trip through the book of Proverbs, written by the wisest man who ever lived. Solomon tells us to acknowledge God in all our ways and He will direct our paths (3:6). He says if we will honor God with our tithes, we will always have plenty (3:9-10). He warns us to raise our children in a godly fashion (22:6). He tells us the things God hates (6:16-19). And he tells us how to attain knowledge and wisdom (chapter 1). Anyone who says life doesn't come with instructions has never read the book of Proverbs.

Genesis tells us all about the creation of the world. (The evolutionists should spend some time here.) Then God tells us the story of the Israelites' release from Egyptian bondage and their 40-year journey through the wilderness to the Promised Land. This is not just another good story. Close observation reveals much of God's character. Why did they wander around for 40 years? I assure you it wasn't because God enjoyed their misery. He was trying to teach them to be grateful for their blessings. He wanted them to see that He was the source of their provision, that only through Him would they find the inner peace for which they were searching. He wanted them to grow up, to give up their selfish ways and their insistence on instant gratification. Though the exodus was thousands of years ago, He wants the same for us today. His Word tells us what they did wrong. It tells us how to avoid the same mistakes.

A reading of the prophets gives us confidence in the inspiration of the Word. There are approximately 6,000 prophecies in the Bible and over 4,000 of them have already come to pass. We are living in the midst of the fulfillment of many more. This tells me I have no reason to doubt that those insights into the last days will be exactly as they are written. No one will be able to say, "But I didn't know."

The New Testament tells us of the life of Jesus and outlines very clearly what we must do to follow Him in this life, and live out eternity with Him in the next life. It tells us of His virgin birth, His short 3-year ministry, His death on the cross for my sins, and His incredible resurrection. I have but to simply believe this and ask Him into my heart and His promises instantly become available to me.

Everything we need to know is between the pages of His book. We have no excuse for not knowing.

He that hath no rule over his own spirit is like a city
that is broken down and without walls.
Proverbs 25:28

When I first read this verse, it was one of those I casually skimmed over, thinking,"Oh, that has no meaning for me personally and therefore doesn't merit my time and attention." I'm ashamed of my selfishness when I am reading the Bible. However, God kept bringing me back to it and I finally put it on my list of verses to memorize, and memorize it I did. But, as is often the case, it took a while for meaning to sink in, and when it did, I was amazed, once again, at the simplicity of God's Word.

In the Old Testament days, walls surrounded all the major cities. The walls were their protection from enemy attack. If there were no walls, invasion and, ultimately, defeat was inevitable.

We are in no less danger of attack today than the people of old were. Actually, our danger is even larger because our greatest enemy does not operate in the physical realm. "... *for we wrestle not against flesh and blood, but against principalities, against powers, against the rulers of darkness of this world, against spiritual wickedness in high places"* (Ephesians 6:12). If we do not have God's protective walls around us, it's an easy matter for the enemy to prance right in and launch an all-out attack against which we have no defense. How do we prevent this crippling disaster in our lives? The above verse tells us we must control our spirit. Okay, that sounds lofty and spiritual, but what does it mean in everyday practical terms?

Controlling our spirit means exercising self-control and self-discipline, those ugly concepts that we sometimes swear were instituted by some crazed sadist. Think again, and read your Bible. The concepts actually come from God. Think you have no self-control or self-discipline? *"For He hath not given us a spirit of fear, but of power, and of love, and of a sound mind"* (2 Timothy 1:7). A sound mind is not possible without self-control and self-discipline, and this verse tells us that God has given these to us as born-again believers.

You may feel you were in the outfield picking daisies the day He was handing out self-discipline. Like every one of His good and perfect gifts, He leaves the choice to us to receive it or not. If our choice is no, we're without protection and the enemy has a wide open shot at us. If our choice is yes, it will require work, but He will be right beside us to help, and as always, when we say yes to Him, the rewards far outweigh the effort.

But his delight is in the law of the LORD; and in his
law doth he meditate day and night.
Psalm 1:2

The practice of scripture memorization has advanced my
spiritual maturity more than anything else, though I can't say
why and I don't know how. I've even been tempted to mark
it off as a coincidence and try to believe that something else
was responsible for the advancement. But it doesn't wash—I
know the truth in my heart.

God tells us throughout the Bible that we are to meditate
on His Word. Joshua 1:8 says if we will meditate on His Word
and do according to all that is written in it, we will make our
way prosperous and have success. What better motivation
could there be? But I have to admit that the understanding of
meditation alluded me for many years. As with many people,
the idea of meditation conjured up visions of sitting cross-
legged in a white robe on the top of a mountain in Tibet. I
actually took some instruction in meditation once, but just
could never get the hang of it (My husband says it's because
I didn't take Humming 101 first).

I'm grateful I was never able to accomplish eastern style
meditation because I don't believe that's what God had in
mind. An empty mind, which is what the eastern style advo-
cates, is an unproductive mind. Supposedly the purpose is
to connect with the higher self, the spirit of the universe. To
me, the spirit of the universe is God, and I can connect with
Him anytime and any place through prayer and His Word.

Putting aside, for the moment, the spiritual aspect of
verse memorization, I was amazed at the practical benefits
of it. In the beginning, it would take me a week to get one
verse down pat, and that was repeating it over and over twice
a day as I rode my stationary bike. Now I can memorize a
verse a day plus repeat all the previously memorized ones
during my exercise periods. An added benefit has been an

improvement in my overall memory, which is no little matter as I enter that time of life when memory becomes an issue.

The greatest benefit, however, *is* a spiritual one. As I ride my bike and quote my scriptures, God brings new meaning and understanding to me. He shows me how I can apply them to my daily life. It has greatly enhanced my prayer life as I can now say with assurance, "You said, God....", and hold Him to his promises. And I can thwart Satan's attacks by flinging the Word at him as Jesus did when He was led into the wilderness to be tempted after His baptism. If it was good enough for Jesus, it's good enough for me.

In the beginning God created the heaven and the earth.
Genesis 1:1

This is the opening statement of the greatest Book ever written. Whereas some verses in the Bible seem to leave themselves open for interpretation (for very good reason, I'm sure), this verse is not one of them. It could not be any clearer.

What do these words do to the theory of evolution? Blows it right out of the water. Unless, of course, you happen to be one of those who picks and chooses the verses you want to believe. Or one of those who doesn't believe in a literal interpretation, but thinks the words were all written in an illusive, figurative fog.

I happen to believe in the literal interpretation for one very good reason. Anytime a writer of the Old Testament was not talking in real time events, they were very careful to say, "I saw this in a dream," or "I had a vision." When Jesus was going to tell a story to make a point, He always prefaced it with, "Here is a parable." So yes, I believe every word just as it was written. That is not to say I like every word of it (there is that "love everyone" thing and also the "wait with patience" admonishment), but I can't pick the best parts and claim them for my own while discarding the rest.

There was a man in my Sunday School class last year whose mind works in the scientific realm. Though definitely a believer in God and a solid Christian, he said he is unable to literally accept parts of the Bible. Specifically, we were talking about God creating the world in six days. His doubt was not that God created the world, but that He did it in six days. He figures days must not have been 24-hours then. But Genesis plainly tells us what God called a day—one morning and one evening (Genesis 1:8). I don't believe the orbits of the sun and moon have changed since He put them in place. I felt sorry for this man, and am very grateful that my mind doesn't work in such a way that I can't accept His Word on faith.

My husband and I have frequently discussed the phenomenon of atheists and evolutionists with their "big bang" theory. It would take a much further stretch of the imagination to go along with that line of thinking than to accept that in the beginning God created the world. Anyone who has studied astronomy and the perfection of the universe with the incredible alignment and everything working together in perfect harmony must know it couldn't have been the result of random circumstances. Or just a cursory look at the amazing way a body functions, or holding a newborn baby will tell you that only a Master could have accomplished it. No, it's not difficult at all for me to believe that, "In the beginning God..."

...I will bless thee and thou shalt be a blessing...
Genesis 12:2

The book, <u>The Prayer of Jabez</u>, by Bruce Wilkinson, took the country by storm. It is based on 1 Chronicles 4:6. It is a simple prayer by a man who is mentioned no where else in the Bible. Basically, he is asking God to bless him, enlarge his borders, and keep him from harm (let's face it, what else do any of us need?).

Jabez's prayer is a prayer of faith. Though containing only 33 words, it displays a faith I wish I could even come close to. It's not the "enlarge my coast" or "keep me from evil" that I want to focus on in this writing. No, it's the "bless me" part.

Jabez doesn't just say, "Bless me." He says, "Bless me indeed." Seems to me that he displayed a lot of audacity. And it's not just an added thought at the end of his prayer. He starts the prayer with this request. It has given me cause to pause and think.

I come from a background that, for many years, I allowed to produce a shame-based nature within me. People who live in this awful pit of shame do not feel they are worthy of anything good and, consequently, will never ask for anything for themselves. In the midst of my pit-dwelling days (which, believe me, will make a person pit-iful), I was extremely self-sacrificing. Or at least I thought I was. I realize now that my self-sacrificing ways were the highest form of selfishness but that's another story for another time. At any rate, I would never buy for myself, take a second helping, or spend time on myself unless and until everyone else in the family was taken care of first. We all know that never happens, so I did without, and I drank.

Even after coming back to God and knowing the shame I claimed was not legitimate, I still have difficulty asking for myself, especially from God. Because of Jesus' work on the cross, I know that I can go boldly to the throne of grace and ask whatever I will. But that boldness is difficult because I can't seem to get past my own unworthiness to focus on the worth of Jesus which covers it. However, the above verse in Genesis has helped me to understand.

I want to serve God. I want to help others. It stands to reason that I can't give away anything I don't have. So yes, God, pour out Your blessings on me so that I may be a blessing to others.

Therefore take no thought, saying, What shall we eat?
or, What shall we drink? or, Wherewithal shall we
be clothed (For after all these things do the Gentiles
seek:) for your heavenly Father knoweth that ye have
need of all these things. But seek ye first the kingdom of
God, and his righteousness; and all these things shall
be added unto you.
Matthew 6:31-33

Until very recently, this verse always completely baffled me. I didn't understand it, but I loved it and had it memorized. It spoke to me in a way I couldn't explain. Somehow I knew it contained the truth that would set me free from worry forever if I could just grasp it.

I've learned something incredible about God. He means what He says. And He says He will reveal His mysteries to us if we will seek Him. As I said, I memorized this verse and quote it twice a day as I do all my memory verses. But I do more than just say the words. I internalize them and use my time of quoting as a prayer. Some verses will be an occasion for thanksgiving because I have seen them as a reality in my life. Some will cause me to think of someone in particular who has been a burden on my heart and I will offer up a prayer for them. Some I love because the words are so beautiful and they eloquently say what I feel but can't find my own words to express. The Psalms especially do this for me. And some cause me to ponder, such as the above verse.

Unlike some of the verses that I simply don't understand and are a source of bewilderment, the above verse puzzled me for a different reason. I understood perfectly what it was saying, I just didn't understand how I was supposed to accomplish it. So I would wonder about it each time I quoted it.

Enlightenment finally came, not as a "aha, eureka!" experience, but more as a slow process. As I pursued my quest of learning about God's principles, ways, and love for me, amazing things began to take place within me. Then came the blessed day I was quoting this scripture and realized I had made it to the core meaning of the words. I truly no longer worried about what we would eat, or drink, or wear for clothing, or any other material thing. Just as the verse says, God already knows my needs and has promised to meet them. If I ever doubt this, I need to learn to discriminate between my needs and my wants. There's no sense in me worrying about those needs, or even giving them a second thought beyond making certain I am a good steward over all He gives. My focus is to be on discovering and learning all I can about Him and developing an ever-growing relationship with Him.

There are many seeming paradoxes in the Bible and this scripture is one of them. As soon as we turn loose of our worries and turn our focus to God, the objects of our concern cease to be an issue.

This book of the law shall not depart out of thy mouth;
but thou shalt meditate therein day and night, that thou
mayest observe to do according to all that is written
therein: for then thou shalt make thy way prosperous,
and then thou shalt have good success.
Joshua 1:8

I am a success junkie. Successful people fascinate me. Please understand, I'm not necessarily talking about material success, though that certainly is one form of it. But there is also success in marriage, parenting, accomplishments, etc. The list is endless.

If I am to believe the statistics (and I've seen enough to have faith in their accuracy), only about 3% of people can be classified as having successful life styles. 3%! Why is that? Do those 3% know something the rest of the world doesn't know? Are they smarter? Do they possess superior abilities? I think not. What makes the difference is persistence; discovering what to do and then doing it until the desired result is attained.

This sounds simple enough, but how do we discover what to do? That's actually the easiest part. The above verse gives us God's very own formula for success. And since it is His, we can be assured that if it is followed, it will work for everyone and without fail. Try to get a guarantee like that from any of the myriad of success manuals that are currently flooding the market.

God's word is His instructions for living an abundant life. Not just a barely get by life. He wants us to be a success, and He tells us very plainly right here how to do it. We are to read His Word. But not just passively read. Meditate on it. Get it into our hearts. Ponder it. Wonder about it. Question it. Pray about it. Make our reading an aggressive, active endeavor. Then start to *"do according to all that is written therein."*

Doing. That was the part I missed for a long time. I filled my head with enough knowledge on success to start my own school. I knew every "right" formula, every required positive attitude, all the proper words. So why wasn't I experiencing any notable measure of success? Oh, there were areas where God had pulled me through quite successfully, such as overcoming my addictions, but there didn't seem to be progress in the everyday areas where I needed victory so badly.

I finally realized that yes, I knew a lot and even had many of the answers, but I wasn't "doing" what I knew to do. With that revelation came the beginning of a tough journey (one I'm still on), putting into action the truths I learn from God's Word. The journey is seldom an easy one, but it is always successful if I stay on the right road.

...for if ye do these things, ye shall never fall...
2 Peter 1:10

Well gee, this is quite a promise. Never fall. I don't like falling. Too much of my life was spent flat on my face as a result of falling, so this really interests me. What are "these things" I must practice so that I will always walk upright? Going back to verses 5-7 gives the answer.

I must apply diligence in my faith. I must have virtue. I must gain knowledge. I must practice temperance, patience, godliness, brotherly kindness, and love. Seems like a pretty tall order and even a little overwhelming if taken all at once. Let's break it down into bite-sized pieces and I believe we'll find it a little easier to swallow.

Diligence in faith. This seems like a mouthful, but it simply means as we are told in Hebrews 10:23 to, *"hold fast the profession of our faith without wavering."* We mustn't have strong faith in the good times and weak faith when we are going through the valley.

Virtue, or moral excellence. This is self-explanatory. Excellence means no compromising. I can't have high standards when it's convenient and toss them aside when faced with strong temptation.

Knowledge. This, I'm certain, refers to the knowledge of God. The only way we can attain this knowledge is to stay in His word. Knowledge and wisdom are not interchangeable. Wisdom is the ability to act on our knowledge and it comes from God. But first we must have that knowledge.

Temperance, or self-control. Another self-explanatory quality. In spite of the excuses we like to give ourselves and others, we do have the ability to practice self-control. It is a part of the Fruit of the Spirit package (Galatians 5:22-23).

Patience. This simply means hanging in there with what we know to be true and right regardless of how the circumstances appear.

Godliness. Allowing God to always work through us will manifest godliness in us. It cannot be accomplished by our own efforts.

Brotherly kindness and love. These two go hand-in-hand. And it doesn't mean just to smile and refrain from ugly words. It means going out of your way to extend your hand when there is a need. Love is an effort. It is not an occasional good deed when you're feeling generous. It is a way of life that never asks, "Do I really feel like doing this?"

Feel that your Christian walk is nothing more than a series of falling over speed bumps? Put these eight qualities to work in your life and see how quickly you are walking upright.

And I saw heaven opened, and behold, a white horse;
and He that sat upon him was called Faithful and
True...
Revelation 19:11

I've never spent much time in the book of Revelations. It's confusing for me as it is for many, but that is no excuse. It is a part of God's word and, as such, deserves the same attention as the rest of the Bible. Maybe even more since it is an account of the end times.

The Book of Revelation was given to the Apostle John in a vision when he was a prisoner on the Island of Patmos. It was given to John by Jesus Christ Himself with instructions to write down everything exactly as he saw in his vision. We can assume with certainty that he did this. Many of the things John described probably made no sense to him, but they are clear to us in light of events that have transpired in the interval between the time it was written and now.

There are many interpretations of the book of Revelation. But the one thing all seem to agree upon is that it is a description of the last days on earth as we know it. Some of the language is frighteningly graphic. One thing that must be observed as the book is read is the words "like" and "as." They indicate a comparison, not an identification. We have to remember that John had only the words he knew to describe the things he saw in his vision. If there was something unknown to him, all he could do was compare it to something he did know.

As I said, I've not read much of the book yet. There was a time I simply didn't want to. It scared me. However, I'm no longer frightened by it because I agree with those who believe most of it is prophecy yet to be fulfilled. I believe the really scary stuff will take place after Jesus has taken the church from the world, so I won't be around to see any of it. I feel sorry for those who will.

There are many who say we're in the last days. I, like everyone else, don't know. And, for myself, I can only say it wouldn't be a bad thing if Jesus came back today. Imagine, as the above verse says, heaven opening and Jesus descending on a white horse. What a glorious sight that will be. Interestingly enough, Revelation 6:2 tells us that the anti-Christ will also be riding a white horse. I suppose his attempts at deception are going to continue right up to the end. No, I don't understand the book, but I do know I am to be about my Father's business and to be ready when the Bridegroom returns for His bride.

*Whereby are given unto us exceeding great and
precious promises: that by these ye might be partakers
of the divine nature, having escaped the corruption
that is in the world through lust.*
2 Peter 1:4

I've been thinking a lot lately about the promises of God. Probably because one of my recent Sunday School lessons was about claiming the promises of God in our prayer life and applying them to our circumstances as a source of hope.

There are over 37,000 promises in the Bible. Now I know that all 37,000 are not for me. For instance, God promised Abraham and Sarah they would have a child at a time when their childbearing years were long past. This promise is not for me (thank You, God), nor would I want to claim it. But besides the obvious, such as this one, how do I know if the promise is one I can claim for myself, or if it was only meant for the people and the circumstance at the time? This has been my dilemma of late.

Another for instance that is not so obvious to me is Joshua 1:8 where God tells Joshua that if he will meditate on the Word and do all that it says, he will be prosperous and successful. Was that promise just for Joshua, or can I claim it for my own? I believe I've found a way to approach this that is satisfactory until and unless God gives me something else.

I have a respectable amount of God-given common sense (though my life has not always reflected that reality). and He expects me to use it. Yes, Joshua 1:8 was a promise given to Joshua. And at first glance it seems to be referring to two unrelated things: meditating on the Word, and prosperity. But reading it with spiritual understanding tells me God meant exactly what He said. So it looks to me like a principle for prosperous successful living for everyone.

The natural person who has no spiritual awareness cannot claim God's promises. In the first place, he wouldn't even want to. They make no sense in the natural. Such as the Joshua verse. Meditating on the Word and success? No way. Or what about Matthew 6:31-33 where Jesus is saying not to worry about food and clothing, but to seek God and His righteousness and all the "things" will be added? Preposterous! No, it takes a person of faith, a child of God, to accept these promises which are often full of seeming contradictions and pure paradoxes.

God's promises are precious and magnificent, just as stated in the above verse. If we will read them with a spiritual eye of understanding and the common sense God gave us, I believe He will reveal which ones we can claim as our own.

And let us not be weary in well doing: for in due
season we shall reap, if we faint not.
Galatians 6:9

The problem with this verse is that it doesn't tell us how long we have to do good before we reap. How long is "due season?" It would have been so much easier had He said, "Do good for one year, five months, and twelve days, then you will begin to reap." Why didn't He do that? I would never presume to second guess God and try to figure out why He does or doesn't do something, but I have a theory about this one. I believe He doesn't tell us how long "due season" is because it is different for each of us. And then there's that doing good thing. My definition of doing good may be totally different from the next person's. For example, I may consider it doing good if I read my Bible every day for a week. The lifelong junkie may think it doing good if he goes a week without shooting up. In a way, we're both right, but getting caught up in those thoughts will cause us to miss the whole point of the verse.

It doesn't matter what my definition of good is, or what your definition is. What matters is God's definition and for that we must go to His Word. We don't have to search far to see that much of what we see as "good" is drawn from society, not from God. Besides the "Thou shalt nots" (which, by the way, are commands, not suggestions), there are numerous good living mandates. If we put Him first in our lives (Matthew 6:33). If we accept the truth of His Son as our Savior (John 3:16). If we acknowledge Him in all our ways (Proverbs 3:6). If we commit our ways to Him (Psalm 37:5). If we meditate on His Word (Joshua 1:8). If we are a good steward with what He gives (Luke 12:42). If we love the unlovely (Matthew 5:44). If we minister to the poor (Proverbs 22:9) and to those in prison (Matthew 25:36). If we have a grateful heart full of thanksgiving (1

Thessalonians 5:18). And the list goes on. These types of things are God's definition of good, not gaining power, accumulating money, achieving fame, having great beauty, or accomplishing more, more, more.

Doing good requires a quiet heart devoted to hearing from God and a determination to immediately obey when He speaks. Doing good may mean taking the time to send a card with a note to that person who is down and needs some encouragement. Or it might mean giving the neighbor who doesn't drive a ride to the post office. I will admit it's not very glamorous by society's standards and not worthy of a write-up in the paper. But it pleases God and that is always to be our goal.

What about the "due season?" Well, that's God's time. If we quit worrying about when we're going to reap and simply focus on the doing good, we'll wake up some morning and realize we're living in the midst of an abundant harvest.

*If ye abide in me, and My words abide in you, ye shall
ask what ye will, and it shall be done unto you.*
John 15:7

In the past, I really latched on to the last part of this verse and others like it. "Ask whatever you wish and it will be done for you" I could almost use as a mantra. I like the promises of God and have always believed them. So I never could figure out why they didn't work for me. Had I missed the verse that said, "All of the promises in My Word are for everyone except Kay?" No, I didn't think so, but I was obviously missing something. What was it?

Finally, I quit doing the "pick and choose" thing, picking and choosing what parts of the verses I liked and wanted for my own while ignoring the rest. When I realized I had to place the pieces I had pulled out back into the context of the whole, it became very clear why the promises had not been working for me. There were conditions attached to them. Almost all of God's promises are what I've come to call "if/then" statements. If I do this, then He will do that.

"But I thought His love was unconditional!" you may want to yell at me. His love is but His promises are not. Even salvation, which the Bible tells us is a free gift, has a condition. The gift is free in the sense that we could never do anything to earn it, but it does come with an "if." If we believe, then we receive. God does not just shower His blessings on everyone without requiring something on our part. The prisons are full of people who never learned the principle of working for what they want. Human nature being what it is, we would all be this type of person if God indiscriminately gave everything to everyone.

The above verse tells me that if I stay close to God and keep His words in my heart, I can ask for whatever I want and get it. You may think that's somewhat of a rash promise. Suppose I decided I wanted a million dollars and the lifestyle that accompanies that kind of money. Well, the truth is, if I fulfill the "if" part of this verse, *"If you abide in me and my words abide in you,"* I'm not going to ask for a million dollars. In Matthew 6: 31-33 He tells me not to worry over "things" but to seek His kingdom and His righteousness and the things will be added. And I know they will be added at exactly the right time and in exactly the right quantity.

This is how the promises work. As long as I do my "if" part, He never fails to come in with His "then" part. It's an incredible way to live.

...God, who giveth us richly all things to enjoy...
1 Timothy 6:17

Some people seem to have the idea that when they come to God, they not only have to give up their worldly possessions, but they also have to forfeit all desires for things. And there are religions (mostly cults) that are more than ready to capitalize on this belief. They exploit the disillusioned, usually the young, who often come from very dysfunctional homes or even orphanages. The religious leaders will send them out to work, taking all of their wages. Or it is the old, who have lost a mate and are lonely and wealthy, who are taken advantage of. All are encouraged to take a vow of poverty and pool their resources for the "good of the group." It's frightening to see how easily these otherwise intelligent people are drawn into this con. I believe it to be an indication of how starved many in our society are to simply feel they belong somewhere.

Though I'm far from being a Bible scholar, I have read through the Book several times. Nowhere do I recall it saying that taking a vow of poverty is going to make a person more holy or bring him closer to God. There are, however, several verses that, if taken out of context, could be used to expound the virtues of being poor.

Jesus said that it is easier for a camel to go through the eye of a needle than it is for a rich man to get into heaven (Matt. 19:24). This puzzling statement was made after a rich man came to Jesus requesting to be one of His followers. Jesus told him to go and sell all of his possessions and then to return and follow Him. The rich man went away sad. I believe this to be the verse the money hungry cult leaders use the most to hook their victims.

A careful reading of the story will reveal that Jesus knew the rich man's heart. He knew that his possessions were the most important thing in the man's life. It does not say we must give up everything to follow God. But we must be willing to give up everything, which is the indication that we put nothing ahead of Him, that He is first in our lives. This is what He is seeking from us—the willingness.

I don't believe God put all of the good stuff: the money, the nice houses, the beautiful cars, the good jobs, etc. out there so that the lost sinners of the world can enjoy them. No, today's verse tells me He intended them for His children to have and enjoy. We just must always remember that there is a fine line between enjoying and coveting. Hold everything loosely.

*Then said the Lord unto me, thou hast well seen: for I
will hasten my word to perform it.*
Jeremiah 1:12

I love this verse. Though I don't normally imagine
in pictures, I do have a vision of God watching over and
protecting His Word, much like a mother hen protects her
nest of eggs. God wrote the Bible, so the words it contains
are literally His words and He personally knows every one
of them.

The last few verses of Revelations (22:18-19) contain a
warning that the words of God's book are not to be added to
or taken from. This tells me that though His original words
have been translated into many languages and often many
times within the same language, He is still watching over it
to perform it. The words in the Bible I read bear little resemblance to the original Greek and Hebrew words of the manuscripts that were the original scriptures. However, the result
is the same. My belief in His Son leads me to salvation just
as promised in His word. All the "if/then" promises work
for me. If I fulfill the conditions He requires, He fulfills His
promises. I can assume He also watches over the English
translation of His word to perform it.

God Himself inspired the original scripture writers to set
in print His very words. So what would be so strange about
a person experiencing that same inspiration to transcribe His
word? As a writer, I have to say it would just about have
to be divine inspiration to motivate a person to undertake
such a monumental task. So, just as He watched over His
words when they were originally written, He now watches
over them each time that they are translated from the original
manuscripts.

God's word is such a miracle. I believe it is divinely
open to interpretation in some areas for a reason. Different
people have different needs at different times. God's word

miraculously speaks to *all* these differences. *Everyone* can find *everything* they will ever need within the pages of the Bible. Now tell me that's not a miracle!

I prayed for God to give me a desire to read His word. That may sound strange, but I wanted to want to and I couldn't seem to get there on my own. He graciously answered that prayer and now my daily reading is a most important part of my life. In His words I find Him, His Son, His love, His goodness, His holiness, His promises, His instructions, His wrath, and I find me. I encourage you to join me in this most exciting adventure.

Stone #7

God's Ways

*Therefore thou shalt keep the commandments of the
LORD thy God, to walk in his ways, and to fear him.*
Deuteronomy 8:6

But they that wait upon the Lord shall renew their
strength: they shall mount up with wings as eagles...
Isaiah 40:31

Wait is the operative word in this verse. In the past, I always envied people who testified to being called by God to their profession, or a project, or a purpose. Without giving it much thought, I assumed if God called a person to something, he stepped into it fully capable, success guaranteed with little or no effort. At least those were my thoughts until God called *me*. I never doubted that it was He who called me because I couldn't have concocted such a wild switch for my life. But then after the shock wore off, the reality of a "calling from God" set in.

The initial calling itself may be other-worldly and on a spiritual plane (I understand He sends angels to beckon some. I was on my way to work sitting at a red light when He called me). However, the actual carrying out of that calling is very much based in the real world of practicality, plans, and hard work. I was naive enough, in the beginning of my venture, to believe that just because God called me, I wouldn't have to do much more than go through the motions and people would beat down my door, begging to do business with me. Ah, silly girl that I was.

God can be very sneaky. Actually, I'm even tempted to use the word devious. When He calls us and plants the dream deep within our hearts, He gives us the vision of the completed work; the successful business, the best seller book, the teacher-of-the-year award, the gold medal, the super bowl ring, "President" lettered on our door, our commercial pilot's license, etc. What He doesn't show us is the journey from where we stand to the realization of that dream. I'm sure He does that for reason, and I suspect that reason is because if we know what all the journey is going to entail, many would give up before ever starting.

For instance, when I first went into recovery, had I seen all my character defects and the work it would take to get them cleaned up, I would have grabbed my bottle and simply drank myself into oblivion. Had I seen the obstacles we were going to face the first year after stepping out and moving cross country, I would never have taken that step. Had I known the work God had to do with me and the amount of time that would lapse before an inkling of success surfaced in my business, I would have closed my ears and ran the red light that day. And if I knew how many thousands of words would have to be written before a book even began to take shape, I would have stuck with reading other people's work. And I would have missed out on so much joy and so many blessings. Wait on God, His plan and His way is the only assurance of success we have.

...let us run with patience the race that is set before us...
Hebrews 12:1

How many times do we hear, "Life is a struggle'? Strangely enough, these words are spoken most often by Christians. Why is that? Paul said in Galations 5:1 that Christ set us free, and Jesus Himself said that He came so that we can have an abundant life (John 10:10). If we are to believe the Bible then these things must be true. So why the struggle? Why the necessity of patience?

The problem of this seeming contradiction lies in the definitions of freedom, abundant life, and struggle. Too often people are led to believe that once they accept Christ as their Savior, life is going to get real easy and all their problems will disappear as they float around on a glory cloud praising God all day. Those who lead people into this misconception do untold harm.

Life does get simpler when we come to God, if we allow it to, but it doesn't get easier. First thing out of the box, Satan is going to attack. He knows the new convert's eternal soul is lost to him, but he's going to do his best to mess up the believer's witness and his life on earth. The Christian who hasn't been warned of this onslaught, and doesn't have a support group helping him to grow and mature in the Word of God, often gets overwhelmed and gives up before getting out of the gate.

The new Christian may think, "Life was a lot easier without God. I didn't have all these problems." And to some extent, he is right. It was easier, but simply because he could go his merry way in total ignorance of his problems. However, once we have Christ in our hearts, His light begins to illuminate the problems, the character defects, the sins, and the uglies (as I call mine). Blissfully ignoring them is no longer an option. (I just realized the association between the words ignore and ignorance which has nothing to do with this, but which I find fascinating.) Once we know something, we can't unknow it.

The struggle and consequent necessity for patience comes into the picture when we make the decision to work with God in getting rid of the uglies. Some may come to this decision immediately. For some it may take years, as it did for me. And some, unfortunately, never arrive at it. They will get to heaven but their heavenly rewards will be few and their life on earth will have no peace, joy, or victory. Don't make the mistake of confusing struggle with unhappiness. Struggle with patience brings victory.

...ask for the old paths, where is the good way, and
walk therein...
Jeremiah 6:16

Our pastor preached a sermon on this verse several weeks ago. I do not recall ever having read it, though I'm sure I have. Probably one of those several times I read through the Bible just so I could say I had done it, but gleaned little from it. At any rate, the verse captured my attention and spoke to my heart in a way I do not yet fully understand. I have ordered the tape of the sermon from my church and intend to listen again to what the pastor said concerning the subject.

God was speaking to the Jews in Judea through the prophet Jeremiah in this verse. So what did he mean, "ask for the old paths?" I don't know. My guess is He was talking about the Israelites' journey to the Promised Land, but I don't know. Perhaps the old paths go all the way back to the Garden of Eden, before the fall of man. The good way was definitely there. And perhaps the "old paths" referred not to one particular time or specific place, but simply to all of the history of time recorded in the scriptures. Certainly the "good way" is woven within the threads of every verse.

Maybe I'm trying to complicate this too much (I have a definite tendency to do this). Perhaps the "old paths" are simply the message that God's will for our life is to love Him and to obey Him. That's what He wanted from Adam and Eve. That's what He wanted from the Israelites. That's what He wanted from the early Christians. That's what he wants from us. If we will do these two things, love Him and obey Him, everything else, and I mean *everything* else, will fall into place. Matthew 6:31-33 tells us that if we will seek first His kingdom and His righteousness, everything else will be added. No one who has access to a Bible can hide behind the excuse that they do not know God's will for their life. It doesn't wash and God won't buy it. I know. I've tried it.

Finding the "good way" for your life is as simple as reading your Bible and meditating on it on a regular basis. I know it's not always easy. I am fortunate enough to have a lot of control over my time and my schedule. Yet, much more often than I like to admit, my focus is on my circumstances, and not on God. I can only imagine how difficult it must be for those with a young family, real jobs, and other outside influences vying for their attention. Difficult, but not impossible. God would never call us to do something that couldn't be done. But we must remember to rely on Him for in our own power it *is* impossible. Read your Bible, find the "good way" and walk in it.

> *...who hath saved us, and called us with an holy*
> *calling, not according to our works, but according to*
> *His own purpose and grace, which was given us in*
> *Christ Jesus before the world began.*
> 2 Timothy 1:9

What a shock it was for me to learn in an "Experiencing God" course that my question to God should be, "What do You want to do through me?" I had always gone to God with *my* plans, *my* list. "Okay God, here's what I'm going to do for You today, and here's what I need to do it. So if You'll hurry and come through with the needs, we can get this show on the road." My method worked just often enough to keep me interested. I know now that those successes probably resulted from me happening on to something God already had in mind for me anyway.

The above verse tells us that God has a purpose for our lives, one that He planned before time began. Other verses throughout the Bible verify this. Now I don't know how long ago "before time began" was, but it's safe to say it was a long time. What makes me, whose lifetime is but a wisp of air, think I'm going to change God's plan for my life? It's not going to happen.

Do I have to follow His plan? No. He's given me a free will and I can exercise it anytime I choose. And I did for many many years, with devastating results. It was certainly not God's will that I spend what should have been the most productive years of my life in the bottom of a bottle. It was not His will that my children's upbringing bred all kinds of emotional and living problems for them. It was not His will that I lived my life as I did. But then, I wasn't too much into starting each morning with an inquiry of what He wanted from me for the day.

When I finally reached the end of my rope and cried out to Him to make some sense of the mess I had made,

He graciously caused *"all things to work together for good"* (Romans 8:28). But it didn't happen instantly for me, as I understand it does for some marvelously blessed people. It's been a process, made incredibly slow at times because of my own reluctance to submit to God's purpose.

I still can't do things in my way. Occasionally He will give me an insight into something new He has for me to do. My excitement and enthusiasm will take over (I love new at least until it's no longer new), and I want to take the ball and run. "Okay God, this is how we'll do this." And I delay the good work He has given me the privilege of performing. But, I'm learning. I know when He gives me something, He has a plan for its accomplishment (1 Thes. 5:24). All I have to do is wait on Him and take it one step at a time and watch His miracles unfold.

Whatsoever He saith unto you, do it.
John 2:5

Jesus' mother said this to the servants at the wedding in Cana. Jesus was about to perform His first recorded miracle: turning the water into wine. Her statement seems pretty simple, but I believe it exemplifies the basic plan for living a godly life.

I've always been one of those people who likes events and I like to see things happen, both for myself and for others. I'm not an idea person; consequently, I'm not much on developing plans. But let someone else make the plan and *then* give it to me, and I'm off and running—the more complicated the better. Even if the plan should start out as a simple one, by the time I get through with it the originator would not recognize it.

Perhaps this is the reason my spiritual progress has been so slow. God's plans, as outlined in the Bible, just seem too simple. I've always secretly felt there must be more to accomplishing abundant living than appears in the words of His Word. I suppose I thought He was giving us the basic outline and it was up to us to furnish all the details. But I believe the Bible is our instruction book for living. Now what kind of product directions would show (A) the parts and (B) a picture of the finished product and leave it up to the purchaser to figure out how to get from A to B? What a mess that would be and soon word would get around and no one would be buying the product. Same thing applies here. If God just told us that we (A—the parts) are to become like Christ (B—the picture of the finished product) and didn't tell us how to accomplish it, it wouldn't be long before all the bearers of the Gospel would be hanging by their toes in the streets.

It's all there in His word. Everything we need to know to get from A to B. And the beauty of it is that it is simple. God doesn't need me to add to or take away anything in His plan. Do I want eternal life? All I have to do is believe in Christ (John 3:16). Do I want prosperity and success? All I have to do is meditate in His word (Joshua 1:8). Do I want to see the glory of God? All I have to do is believe (John 11:40). Do I want wisdom? All I have to do is ask God (James 1:5). Do I want the peace of God that defies understanding? All I have to do is be anxious for nothing, pray, and give thanksgiving (Philippians 4:4-7). Do I want all things to work together for my good? All I have to do is love God and be called according to His purpose (Romans 8:28). Do I want the desires of my heart? All I have to do is delight myself in the Lord (Psalm 37:4). Do I want my paths to be straight? All I have to do is commit my ways to Him (Psalm 37:5). And the list goes on and on. Just as the opening verse states. Do I want miracles in my life? All I have to do is whatever He says.

The current trend across America is to simplify our lives. Try God's way. It doesn't get much simpler than this and the rewards are literally out of this world.

*Enter ye in at the strait gate...because strait is the gate,
and narrow is the way, which leadeth unto life and few
there be that find it.*
Matthew 7:13-14

The path of the Christian life is narrow indeed. Which is, of course, the reason so many are hesitant to set out on it. When those who are of the world consider coming to God, they think only of the things they will have to give up. This thought frightens many while simply turning off others.

Are there things that must be relinquished in order to live the righteous life demanded of God's children? You bet there are — many of them. But, surprisingly, the entrance to the narrow path is not always narrow. God is gracious in not yanking the rug from beneath us all at once. He knows that could be overwhelming.

Though I was saved at a young age, I didn't actually embark on that narrow path until God pulled me from the throes of alcoholism in my mid-forties. When I quit drinking, had I seen everything God would be requiring of me, I would have thrown up my hands and said, "It's impossible, no way can I do that," and crawled right back in the bottle. But in His wisdom, as I took that first step onto the path, all I had to do was not drink. And I didn't even have to do that forever, just one day at a time.

As time went by, He started bringing up the other addictions. First there was the smoking, then the gambling. Next came the overeating, and hot on its trail was the overspending. Soon (well, not really soon, some we are still working on) all the gross, outwardly noticeable things were mostly conquered. I was feeling pretty smug about my victories, but it was not a state in which He allowed me to stay. I discovered the bad habits and addictions I had labeled "big" were minor compared to the flaws He began to uncover.

I had to give up my controlling attitude and allow everyone to live their own lives, make their own mistakes, and suffer their own consequences. I had to quit coming up with excuses to justify the things I wanted to do but that I knew in my heart were wrong. I had to quit compromising my values when they got in the way of my desires. I had to acknowledge and accept my uniqueness instead of always comparing myself unfavorably with others.

Is this an all-inclusive list and have I arrived? Hardly. Each time I think I'm "there" God springs something new on me. I've finally realized I will never arrive—not in this lifetime. And that's okay. As long as I'm going forward, that's progress. Narrow? Yes, but the blessings He bestows far outweighs anything I've had to give up in the journey. After all, the things He required me to give up only gave me misery anyway.

*...neither are your ways my ways saith the Lord...for as
the heaven are higher than the earth, so are my ways
higher that your ways...*
Isaiah 58:8-9

We should never limit God to our feeble ways or our small thinking. When we do, we deny ourselves many of His blessings. My entire life has been a testimony to this fact.

My husband and I are currently in the process of moving to a different house. Several of the rooms in the new house needed painting, and in my usual impulsive manner, I boldly announced, "Let's buy the paint and I will do it myself." The most painting I had ever done was maybe some touch up on woodwork. But what I lacked in knowledge and ability, I made up for in enthusiasm.

Monday morning finds me at the new house asking God to help me do a good job, fully expecting Him to do just that. Fortunately, He knows more about my limitations than I do. I had painted less than one wall when reality set in. My arthritic hands were hurting so bad I realized there was no way I was going to be able to finish the job.

As I sat on the floor nearly crying from frustration, my husband came in with one of the laborers from his job. His boss had told him to take the laborer and spend the day painting. They were completely done by 2:30 that afternoon. It would have taken me a month. Some would say my prayer of, "Please help me to do a good job" wasn't answered. Not so. Sometimes we don't pray correctly because we're limiting God to our small thinking. But fortunately, He often answers what we *should* pray instead of what we *do* pray. In this instance, His answer was to the more appropriate prayer of, "Please help this paint job to get done."

We learn this more appropriate way to pray as we mature spiritually. For years I prayed for my husband to quit drinking. I was certain if that would happen, then I would quit drinking and our lives would magically change. I was so focused on making him change that God couldn't work with me on the real problem—my own drinking. Years were wasted because I limited Him to my thinking and was praying for the wrong things. He stayed out of my way, giving me enough rope to hang myself. Once I did hang myself (figuratively), and knew I had to quit drinking, my husband followed me in sobriety eight months later.

It's amazing what God can accomplish in our lives when we give Him free reign and seek only His will through our prayers. He wants to bless us and show us His power, His ways, and His thoughts, but He won't force Himself on us. We have to be willing to ask for and receive His best.

*Let your light so shine before men, that they may see
your good works, and glorify your Father which is in
heaven.*
Matthew 5:16

Our oldest daughter, who is currently incarcerated in a
state prison, called us yesterday evening, excitement obvious
in her voice. She had been privileged to be used by God to
help lead someone to Christ. It started several months ago
when the young lady approached our daughter and asked her
how she managed to stay calm, peaceful, and serene in the
midst of the turmoil in which they live. Our daughter simply
raised her Bible, which she happened to be reading, and said,
"This is how." That began a series of discussions, readings,
questions, and answers culminating yesterday in the sinner's
prayer. Our daughter, on a natural high that her drugs of the
past couldn't touch, said, "Oh Mom, I could really get used
to this."

I believe most Christians have the mistaken idea of the
obligation in leading others to Christ. We think if we're not
preachers, teachers, or evangelists, there *is* no obligation.
While we are not all called to be Billy Grahams, as the above
verse tells us, we are to let God's light shine through us in
such a way that others are drawn to Him. Leading others to
Christ is *every* Christian's obligation.

Letting God's light shine through her is exactly what our
daughter does. She never pounds anyone over the head with
her Bible, but by the same token, she is never ashamed to
let anyone see her reading it. She doesn't push her beliefs
off on anyone, but is bold in proclaiming them when asked
and doesn't apologize for them. She doesn't grab people and
tell them the sinful road to destruction they're traveling, but
she also refuses to get caught up in the confusion of their
chaos. The outward signs of peace and joy that result from

His work in her life do the talking. And it's effective as her phone call yesterday proves.

I've heard it said that people today aren't reading their Bibles, they're reading Christians. That's true. Just tell someone you're a Christian, or put a spiritual bumper sticker on your car, or wear a Jesus pin. People will start watching you. They want to know if you truly are different and, if so, how. They will be quick to condemn you for the very things they themselves do because they *want* you to be different. I personally would prefer people not advertise their Christianity if they're going to act like the rest of the world. If you're not going to take care of your car and keep it clean, don't put a bumper sticker on it saying how much you love Jesus. Don't wear a pin that says, "Smile, Jesus loves you" if you're going to be impatient and rude in the grocery store line. Act in such a way that people will see the light of God shine through you and they will want what you have.

*Is not this the fast that I have chosen to loose the bands
of wickedness, to undo the heavy burdens, and to let
the oppressed go free, and that ye break every yoke.*
Isaiah 58:6

Today I am beginning what I believe will be a three-day
fast. I've not had a lot of experience with fasting; only a
couple of one-day fasts and one which lasted two days. This
will be my first three-day one.

My first fast originated from a true holy desire to be
closer to God. I don't think this can be accomplished in
only one day, at least not for me, but it is a good exercise in
self-discipline. The other fasts were to lose weight, though
I convinced myself my motives were more pure. And what
about this one? My goal is the above verse, *"to loosen the
bands of wickedness, to undo the heavy burdens, and to be
let the oppressed go free..."*

The purpose of fasting seems to be to get closer to God.
It is usually coupled with prayer in His word. It certainly
is not something I understand, but it appears to be a source
of power. In the 17th chapter of Matthew, the disciples ask
Jesus why they were unable to help a demon-possessed
person. Jesus tells them that kind of action requires prayer
and fasting. If there is more power available to me from God,
I surely want to be able to access it.

This particular fast has to do with my eating (seems
appropriate, doesn't it?). I had gained what I believed to be
victory over my eating problem through a wonderful eating
program God brought to me at just the right time. It is based
on spiritual principles and brought me down to nearly my
desired weight. But then the holidays happened; I caught a
cold, was unable to exercise, and suddenly I no longer had
control over anything.

It is my prayer that this fast will bring me back, mentally,
to where I need to be. I desire that God will reveal to me

something that will help me to break off the yoke of bondage in this area, and to loosen the bonds of wickedness. Some people may think that phrase seems a little extreme when discussing over-eating, but it isn't. Satan uses whatever he can, whatever is available, whatever the vulnerable spot is. For me it is eating, and he attacks mercilessly. But God tells me He will not let me be tempted beyond what I can bear and will provide a way out for me (1 Cor. 10:13). This is my goal—to find a way out that will work consistently when Satan launches his attacks.

...and yet I shew unto you a more excellent way.
1 Corinthians 12:31

God doesn't like mediocrity. So why is there so much of it in the world? Because of laziness and apathy. Excellence takes effort, caring, and desire.

Doing things in an excellent manner is not a quality we are born with. But that's good news because it means we can learn it at any stage of life. Granted, it's easier to learn at a young age rather than later in life, as is everything, but it's never too late. I know because I embarked on my lessons in excellence at an age well past youth.

It helps to have an example while learning anything and excellence is no exception. My example has been my husband. My first real personal, up close experience with his excellence, and what consequently started me on my own path in that direction, was when we built our house in Texas. Those who helped us work on it frequently commented that they would be there seeking shelter in the event of a hurricane. Everything, and I mean everything down to each nail, was meticulously planned and carried out. Strangely enough, even the alcohol, which was so much a part of his life at that time, didn't dim his abilities or his commitment to excellence.

I did not grow up with excellence and did not learn it early in life. Though excellence was not a quality I possessed, I was a perfectionist. This seems like a paradox but these contradictory qualities did not cause conflict for me. If I couldn't do something perfectly, as was usually the case, I simply wouldn't do it at all. Perfection and excellence are not the same thing and I had to learn this in my quest.

Though I was also still drinking when we built the house (and unlike my husband, the alcohol *did* affect my abilities and commitment), that was when I began to learn excellence and the difference between it and my perfectionism.

When mistakes were made or if something didn't quite come together as he planned, my husband would simply take time out to re-figure, re-plan, and re-work it all together for the good. I was great at starting things but if they didn't work out, I would just throw the baby out with the bath water and scrap the whole thing.

God calls us to be excellent in all we do. I've learned through watching and listening to my husband that in the long run excellence is the easiest and simplest way to go. This shouldn't be surprising since God's way is always the simplest way. Think about it. How many things have you had to go back and redo because you didn't take the time to do it right in the first place?

Ye have compassed this mountain long enough...
Deuteronomy 2:3

God spoke this to the Israelites as they journeyed through the wilderness. Perhaps they had come to a place they felt was sufficient. Maybe it wasn't great, wasn't the land of milk and honey, but it was okay. And God allowed them to stay for awhile, but then it was time to move on. Ever get to a point in your life where things are reasonably good and you're pretty comfortable? Oh, things could be better and you know it but it seems the increase in quality is not favorably proportionate to the effort required to make it happen. So you decide to just stay at the mountain.

God, however, doesn't seem to be interested in what we consider to be "favorably proportionate" and He won't leave us alone on the mountain. He simply will not leave us in a comfortable place for long before He starts to call us to ever-higher levels. His call is subtle at first—easy to miss if we're not super sensitive to the promptings of the Holy Spirit. It's just a vague idea that pops into the mind. If you're like me, you might say, "Now where did that come from?" You quickly dismiss it because, chances are, it's something that's going to require some time and effort on your part and very often some sacrifice. That's seldom appealing when we have a heartfelt desire to follow and please God. It's very easy to ignore those first inklings as nothing more than random thoughts that we hope will die from lack of encouragement.

However, God is not so easily put off. Soon the same thought is back, only with greater clarity. It flits in and out of the mind at the most inopportune moments until it finally reaches an intensity that is impossible to ignore.

This is how I've come to recognize if something is from God. It's not 100% infallible but it is an incredibly accurate measure. If an idea is one of my own, I find it difficult to maintain any degree of enthusiasm. I can't seem to make a plan come together for its accomplishment and it soon dies a natural death. But if the idea is from God, it simply won't go away. I stay excited about it even when there seems to be no reason for excitement. It's not uncommon for supernatural circumstances to come together for the accomplishment against all odds.

Why won't God let us stay at the mountain? Well, it certainly isn't because He needs us to do His work. It must be because He loves us and wants us to experience all the blessings He has for us.

God created man in his own image
Genesis 1:27

There have been an estimated 12 billion people in this world since Adam and Eve (half of whom are alive today). I find it incredible that each one has been unique and different. In the first place, my mind has difficulty comprehending 12 billion anything, much less 12 billion variations on the same thing. If nothing else ever did, this certainly speaks to the awesomeness of God. He must truly love variety.

The Bible tells us we are to celebrate the differences in man, to love each one for whom he is, and not to judge him. (Please understand, that does not mean we have to excuse unacceptable behavior.) As John F. Kennedy said, "The family of man is more than three billion strong (true at that time). It lives in more than one hundred nations. Most of its members are not white. Most of them are not Christian. Most of them know nothing about free enterprise or due process of law." Those of us who are white Christians, knowledgeable of free enterprise and due process of law, and living in the United States need to remember this.

Man is such a miracle. Just the composition and the construction of the body with all the muscles, bones, organs, nervous system, circulatory system, etc. staggers the mind. And what about the mind? No one has any idea what it is capable of, for no one has come close to using its full potential or capacity. I've often wondered why God made the brain with such immense capabilities when man only scratches the surface of its use. I once read that the possible connections in the brain are estimated to be a 1 with 2 million miles of typewritten zeros behind it. Since that estimate was made, however, scientists have decided there is no limit to the number.

God also placed within the body the amazing ability to heal itself. I think about the damage I did to myself (physically, mentally, emotionally, and spiritually) through 32 years of hard drinking. That my body is now superbly healthy in all four of these areas (though there are those who question the mental condition) is the stuff of which miracles are made. Think about this: every eight weeks I donate a pint of blood. In a very short time my body manufactures another pint of brand new blood. How does it do that?

I believe we all need to occasionally pause and contemplate the miracle of our bodies and take the time to be grateful to God for that miracle. Don't wait until you lose the use of some portion of it to appreciate it.

Six days thou shalt work...
Exodus 34:21

I frequently write about my parents in negative terms concerning their alcoholism, etc., but I usually do this in the context of making a point. They certainly were not all bad. One thing I learned from them that has served me well all through my life was their work ethic. They believed in working for what they got and they both worked hard.

Well, I have to say, maybe my dad didn't work so hard while he was drinking, but I remember those times when my mother worked hard enough for both of them. She cleaned motel rooms, worked on an assembly line in a glove factory, and labored in a dry cleaners. She finally got a job in an insurance office that she kept for 25 years until she took early retirement to raise a grandson and great-grandson. I remember when she first started that job. My dad was in prison, leaving her the sole support of my brother and me. There was no such thing as government aid to dependent families at that time, and she probably wouldn't have accepted it if it had been available. She would walk to and from work each day (six miles round trip) because she didn't have the dime it cost to ride the bus. One day, as we were down to nothing to eat in the house, she found a ten-dollar bill while walking home. God does provide, doesn't He?

At any rate, because of my parent's influence, I too have been a hard worker all my life. Even at the height of my own alcoholism I received an award for five years perfect attendance on my job (I had to feel that some part of my life was working). My husband has also been a responsible, conscientious, hard worker all his life, including throughout his own heavy drinking years. Consequently, this is something we passed on to our children. (Perhaps the only good thing.) None are lazy and all three work hard and have always been gainfully employed. This is something I took for granted until I started listening to other parents talk about how lazy their grown children are or how they can't (or won't) hold a job. I'm very grateful for my children.

God did not intend for us to have something for nothing. As 2 Thessalonians 3:10 says, "...if any would not work, neither should he eat." It doesn't get much plainer than that. I'm grateful to my parents for the work values they instilled in me.

Doeth not even nature itself teach you...
1 Corinthians 11:14

The Bible says God speaks of Himself to everyone through nature. There was a time when I would have questioned the validity of that statement. That, however, was the time of my life I would have questioned anything on a spiritual level. Thank God, I don't now.

Nature is proof positive of God's love of variety. I live in the desert and marvel at the beauty of it. I have also lived by the ocean, which is equally beautiful, though I didn't have the sense to marvel at it at the time. I do not believe there is a place on earth that does not have within it some inherent beauty.

My husband and I were in Hawaii a couple of years ago and the beauty there is indescribable. The sea is a clear blue and boasts a variety of fish the colors of which I've never seen before. There are beds of coral that team with sea life and hint of untold treasures. There are brilliant flowers blooming everywhere, and the wild are as beautiful as the landscaped. It's my understanding this incredible place was born from volcanic action. What a miracle!

There is a rhythm in nature that man would be wise to study and adopt. As Ecclesiastes 3:1 tells us, *"To everything there is a season."* The moon regulates the ocean; the tides go in and the tides go out, always on schedule, never early, never late. The trees sprout new leaves, grow, shed those leaves, and seemingly die only to burst forth with new growth in the spring.

The wild animals each have their own time and rituals for mating, bringing forth their new life right on schedule. And as the new are born, the old finish out their assigned cycle and die. We humans are the only ones that don't live our lives according to the rhythm of nature. We don't sleep when we're tired and we eat when we're not hungry. Only we, and the dogs that we have domesticated, overeat. Think about it. Have you ever seen a fat tiger or an overweight mouse? And why do we insist on regular mealtimes? We should eat only when we're hungry and only until we're full. We are also the only species to suffer from stress. Have you ever seen a bird in a tree having a nervous breakdown?

Look at the word natural. It is derived from the word nature. We could go a long way in life if we would just take our clues from nature and live in a natural way.

Then I went down to the potter's house, and, behold, he
wrought a work on the wheels, and the vessel that he
made of clay was marred in the hand of the potter; so
he made it again another vessel, as seemed good to the
potter to make it.
Jeremiah 18:3-4

There is an old hymn that says, "You are the potter, I am the clay. Make me and mold me, for this I pray." These are beautiful words and while we're in church, we sing them with what we believe to be heartfelt sincerity. But then we get away from the spiritual setting of the sanctuary and the beautiful voices of the choir, and go out into the world. God puts us on the potter's wheel and after the first couple of spins, life starts to get real uncomfortable and we yell, "Let me off of here!" So we jump off and go back to leading our quiet little lives of desperation, wondering why we never experience any kind of spiritual breakthrough.

We all want to be different, but no one wants to change. We may sing the song correctly, but what we're really thinking is, *I am the potter, You are the clay. Let me mold You and make You to do my bidding.* We have it in our mind what we want to be, and we want God to give us a holy zap and turn us into that person. But it simply doesn't work that way.

First of all, we have to reconcile ourselves to the fact that maybe, just maybe, what we have in mind for ourselves is in no way related to the plan God has for us. At one time, I saw myself as a stylish sophisticated corporate executive, jetting around the world solving problems for my company. My reality, doing what I believe God wants me to do, is sitting in my little home office in my jeans, sweatshirt, and tennis shoes, pouring over a writing in an effort to capture God's will for my readers on paper.

After we've surrendered our dreams to God and, from the heart, desire only His plans for us, it's time to climb up on the potter's wheel and ask the Potter to go to work. This is not a casual experiment for the wishy-washy. A firm commitment must be made to stay on the wheel, no matter how much pain is involved or how much discomfort is experienced. There are two things to keep uppermost in our mind as we are being pushed, pulled, stretched, formed, and molded by the Master Potter. 1) He will never give us more than we can bear (1 Corinthians 10:13), and 2) His chastening is for our good (Hebrews 12:10).

I can't say how long a person must stay on the wheel. I have a theory that may be disconcerting to some, but I hope does not discourage any. My theory is that it may be a lifetime thing, which is what I foresee for myself, anyway. Oh, we do reach the point where the big, difficult, excruciatingly painful parts are over, but He always wants to be doing the fine-tuning and refining that gets us ever closer to the image of His Son.

*Lo, children are an heritage of the Lord: and the fruit
of the womb is his reward.*
Psalm 127:3

Parenthood. I don't feel qualified to write on this topic. Sure, I have three children, but just "having" children does not make a person a parent.

I've often wondered at God's wisdom in giving children to the young. Of course, there is the sheer physical requirement to think about, and I will be the first to admit that it is no small consideration. But it seems that it is not until we are old enough to be grandparents that we even begin to acquire enough knowledge and experience to raise a child (perhaps that is why God made grandparents).

In earlier times it was easier to raise children. The entire family: kids, parents, grandparents, aunts, uncles, and cousins lived close to each other, if not in the same house. The child was surrounded by people who loved him, and were always quick to correct him. He had school to contend with and chores to be done. There was not enough time to get into trouble. Even if there had been, some adult with eyes in the back of their head was always lurking near by. Or a cousin and/or sibling was present, just hoping for the opportunity to tattle.

Today Mom and Dad are wrapped up in their careers. They are seldom home, and when they are, they have neither the time nor the inclination to bother with the children. They leave the oh-so-necessary training of values to the daycare centers and the schools, both of which are forbidden by the government to teach things like values. They might get a bare minimum of exposure to these values in Sunday school and church, but, after all, Sunday is Mom and Dad's only day off. They can't be expected to get up early, dress up, and then go spend half the day in church.

I wonder why these people even want children. And a surprising number of them are opting not to. Though I find that many of these couples are selfish, materialistic people, at least they are being responsible in admitting they don't want the trouble, expense, and bother of children. I'm glad of this because we don't need that particular gene pool expanded.

No, having children does not make a parent. What does make a parent is someone (and this doesn't have to be the person who "had" the child) who is willing to read and follow the instructions. You didn't know children came with instructions? Absolutely! Read the book of Proverbs sometime.

Watch and pray, lest ye enter into temptation. The
spirit truly is ready, but the flesh is weak.
Mark 14:38

"If the world were merely seductive, that would be easy. If it were merely challenging, that would be no problem. But I rise in the morning torn between a desire to save the world and a desire to savor the world. That makes it hard to plan the day." This quote is by E. B. White, the author of the great children's book, <u>Charlotte's Web</u>. I can definitely relate to what Mr. White says. My definition of temptation is a force that lures or beckons a person into an activity or thought which is morally wrong for him. And I emphasize the "for him" because, while there are certain moral wrongs that apply to everyone such as the Ten Commandments; there are other areas that are individually specific. For instance, I have a weight problem and since I know it is God's will for me to be as healthy and to look as nice as possible, it is morally wrong for me to eat a piece of chocolate cake. On the other hand, someone who does not have a weight problem and for whom sugar is not a health issue, chocolate cake can be an everyday part of their life (and oh how I envy those people).

Resisting temptation is a simple matter. Notice, I said simple, not easy. The first step is knowing right and wrong. There are several ways this is accomplished. First of all, God tells us in His word that He put the knowledge of Himself in our beings before we were ever born. To know Him is to instinctively know right from wrong. We may have deeply buried this knowledge by searing our consciences, but it is still within our beings and can be accessed.

Ideally, we had loving, nurturing parents who taught us right from wrong as we were growing up, but that's not always the case. Taught, or teach, is the operative word here. Most parents just want to tell their children what they should do, but children are smart and don't buy into the mixed messages. A parent can't tell a child to be honest and then turn around and brag to the neighbor about cheating on his income tax. I once heard, "Who you are speaks so loud I can't hear what you say." Children need for their parent's actions to be consistent with their words. They are going to follow what they see not what they hear.

The other way we learn right from wrong is by reading the Bible. People often say it's a shame life doesn't come with instructions. It does. Everything we need to know about living a full joyous life is contained within God's word, including how to resist temptation.

As I said in the beginning, resisting temptation is simple. First determine what is right, then as the ads say about drugs, just say no to that which is wrong. Choosing right over wrong is not always easy, and it's not always the choice we want to make. But it is always simple.

And we know that all things work together for good
to them that love God, to them who are the called
according to His purpose.
Romans 8:28

This is my favorite verse in the Bible. It was the subject of our ladies' Bible study yesterday morning. As the class opened, our teacher read the verse and then asked, "How many of you truly truly believe that everything in your life works together for the good?" I was quick to raise my hand (I'm not sure, but I believe I may have been the only one in the group who did). And it suddenly dawned on me that I *do* believe it. I'm very grateful for the conviction, the belief, and finally, the realization.

So, am I Ms. Super Spiritual and that is the reason for my firm conviction? Hardly. But God did bless me with one gift which I feel is necessary for a person to latch onto and claim this verse for their own life. That gift is a positive attitude. With the aid of this great blessing, I'm able to see the good in every single situation. And yes, it does exist in all of them. Maybe I don't see it at the exact moment the storm is raging, but I always see it in retrospect.

I was sexually abused as a child. You may wonder how anything good could possibly come from that. Well, according to the above verse, it is possible. Not only possible, but a reality. Because of that sexual abuse, it's very easy for me to recognize the behaviors that are a result of abuse in others. I am then able to put my arm around them and let them know I understand. Sometimes God leads me to tell my own story, sometimes to just offer a prayer. Our oldest daughter revealed to us several years ago that she too had been sexually abused as a child. Because of my own experience I was able to give her the comfort she needed. And I was also able to know that she could get past it. That is not something I could have believed without having lived it.

My past was filled with many addictions—my own and those of my family. I swam in a sea of vodka for 32 years before God mercifully reached down and pulled me out as I was going down for the third time. Even this most awful condition He caused to come together for the good. I've been sober a number of years now and it is still an awesome miracle to wake each morning without a hangover. Most people take small things like this for granted, but they are cause for me to fall to my knees in gratitude. If I hadn't lived in the pits of purgatory, my life wouldn't be filled with these constant sources of joy and wonder now.

Yes, God does cause all things to come together for the good. Even my things, as terrible as they have been. Even your things.

For God hath not given us the spirit of fear; but of
power, and of love, and of a sound mind.
2 Timothy 1:7

William Menninger, co-founder of an early twentieth century behavioral disorders treatment center, once said, "Mental health problems do not affect three or four out of every five persons, but one out of one." I agree with him. We all have mental health problems. To what degree is the only question for each individual.

Psychiatry is a comparatively new study and science. It is far from being perfected. I heard somewhere that the mind is the final frontier. In other words, it is the last place in the universe to explore and conquer. Because it is not tangible, however, I do not believe we will ever unravel all the mysteries it contains.

Why is one person reasonably balanced with quality mental health while the person next to him, and often it is a member of the same family, may be a psychotic killer? As with everything, theories abound. Actually, there may be more theories in this area than other areas simply because of the intangibility. The truth is, I don't think anyone knows. Some say there is a chemical imbalance in the brain of the severely mentally disturbed. Some claim it is a childhood trauma that triggers the disorder. I've always wondered about *that* particular theory. If it's true, why doesn't everyone who experiences similar childhood trauma have the same problem?

Lawrence J. Peter, formulator of the Peter Principle concerning competence in hiarchical organizations, said, "Psychiatry enables us to correct our faults by confessing our parent's shortcomings." Unfortunately, this is all too common in the mental health field. The professionals are giving a whole society an excuse to avoid responsibility and continue in bad behaviors.

Family therapist and feminist, Maryanne Walters, is of the opinion that, "The point of therapy is to get unhooked, not to thrash around on how you got hooked." What difference does it make *how* you got where you are? The question is, what are you going to do to change it? I've never met anyone who had a perfect childhood. No, I take that back. I did know one person who said she had a perfect childhood and she was the most boring person I've ever known. We all have things from our past to overcome because we deal with people and people are imperfect and make mistakes.

God has placed a desire in my heart to work with those who seem to have lost touch with their spirit and soul: the imprisoned, the addicted, the homeless. I believe the message He wants me to carry to them is that they are *not* broken — maybe badly bent, but not broken. God has given them the power to overcome and it all begins in the mind. The formula is the same for them as it is for all of us, which is to accept the responsibility for where we've been, where we are, and where we're going, commit to changing the bad behaviors, then leave it in God's hands and follow His guidance.

Stone #8

Faith

⁓

For we walk by faith, not by sight
2 Corinthians 5:7

*So then faith cometh by hearing, and hearing by the
word of God.*
Romans 10:17

Romans 12:3 tells us, "*as God hath dealt to every man
the measure of faith.*" So no one can say they do not
have any faith. It may be small and it may be buried under
a bunch of garbage, but it's there. We have God's assurance
of that.

How do we increase our faith? Just how do we get to
that place where we can turn our problems over to God and
trust that whatever He does with them is in our best interest?
I wish I had a step-by-step method but I don't. All I can do
is share my journey of faith with you and tell you how it has
been for me. And I'll tell you right up front that it's been a
process, not an event. A very slow process at times.

My first step into the spiritual realm of faith was the
night I hit bottom in my alcoholism. That is often the starting
place for the addicted. For some reason, I had to come to
the very end of my rope, my own resources, my abilities,
before I turned to God, and I think that is true of many. And,
of course, He knows this and though I'm sure it's not His
preferred method, He allows it so that we *will* reach out for
Him.

God took me as I was: sick, broke, tired, and scared.
He gently picked me up, dusted me off, and set me on firm
ground. I certainly wasn't too firm in the beginning, but the
path He called me to was. He taught me, one day at a time,
to take care of things as they came up and not to look at the
whole picture or too far into the future.

In the beginning, my life was such a mess I had no choice
but to trust Him. I had backed myself into a corner with my
bad choices and many of the messes had no apparent solutions. God took control and I had to let Him. One by one, He

unraveled the complications and I started to believe there might be some hope. It was through these first several years when I *had* to have faith that I learned to have faith.

I'm sorry to say that even with so much evidence of His faithfulness, my faith grew slowly. It was difficult for me to turn things over to Him when I felt I could or should take care of them myself. And frequently he would let me try— always with less than desirable results.

The above verse tells us that faith comes by hearing and hearing by the Word of God. There is no way our faith can grow outside the Word of God. How can we have faith in someone we don't know? And how can we know Him if we don't go to the source? The more we read the more we learn. The more we learn the greater our faith. It's that simple.

*...if ye have faith as a grain of mustard seed, ye shall
say unto this mountain, remove hence to yonder place;
and it shall remove...*
Matthew 17:20

Jesus said this to His disciples when they asked Him why they had been unable to heal a sick man and drive the demons from him. Jesus admonished them, explaining that their lack of faith was the reason for their ineffectiveness. I've always looked at these verses in the same way many people do — incorrectly. In the early pre-dawn of one of my morning devotions, God opened my eyes to the truth of faith.

As is my usual way, I had taken one of God's simple basic concepts, faith, and complicated it beyond recognition. The Bible tells me that through faith I can have salvation, which is, of course, the greatest gift we receive from God. I have no problem with that and accept the reality of my salvation totally, without hesitation or doubt. But the blessings of faith don't end with our salvation experience. On the contrary; that is only the beginning.

The Bible further tells me that through my faith I can receive joy, peace, contentment, prosperity, wisdom, knowledge, love, compassion, and on and on the list goes, including, as the above verse states, the ability to move mountains. And I have achieved a certain amount of all of these in my life, but just not in the amounts I desire or that I feel His word promises.

So what is the problem? I've always seen it as a lack of faith on my part. If I could just somehow build my faith to the proper amount, then God would look down and say, "Okay Kay, you've finally accomplished enough faith. Now you can go out and accomplish all these things and start moving mountains." (Notice what I said here. *I* could accomplish. *I* could move mountains.) My real difficulty with this whole idea, however, is that I just didn't know how to get this proper amount of faith or even what the proper amount of faith was.

Enter God with two short sentences in my devotional book. "We can never gain enough faith in our own abilities to live a godly life. Our faith must be in God to produce it through us." As I said, simple, but oh so profound for me. I don't have to do or get any of the things I seek, the peace and joy and prosperity and goodness. I know now that I'm not capable, which explains my inability in the past to increase my faith in any area. It's not me—it's God. My faith is that He can and will do it through me. I can quit all the struggling and just allow Him the freedom. As the above verse states, I am to say to the mountain, "Remove." It doesn't say I am to remove the mountain. That's God's responsibility. My responsibility is simply to believe that He will do it. I have a feeling life is about to get much easier for me.

Whereof he hath given assurance unto all men...
Acts 17:31

I occasionally feel sorry for people who operate predominately from a left brain scientific point of view. For instance (I read a quote which correctly stated that, "for instance" or "for example" is not proof positive), there is a man in my Sunday morning Bible study class who admits that his scientific mind inhibits him from accepting a literal interpretation of the Bible. He says he simply cannot accept that the earth and all therein was created in six days. I find this sad.

AA states in their *Big Book* that it is the more intelligent people who have trouble applying the program. I believe this may also be true of the great truths of the Bible and God's awesome plan of salvation. Why would these things baffle the highly intelligent? Because the plans and revelations are too simple for the educated mind to believe in their truth or effectiveness. It seems the less educated a person is, the more he can accept on pure faith. This is not purely theory on my part. It is based on much observation and credible periods of time spent with people of all levels of intelligence.

I can recall an instance shortly after I entered recovery when I was struggling with getting past something negative that was going on in my life, but over which I had absolutely no control. For two days I agonized over my options, analyzing the situation from every angle and playing out a hundred "what ifs" in my mind. One day, in the middle of this mental anguish, I was reading the *Big Book*. It said, "If you have a problem, give it to God." Just that plain, just that simple. Had I read it two or three days earlier, I would have dismissed it thinking, *yeah, well, you don't know about my problem.* But God had allowed me to go through all of my complicated mental gymnastics so that I could accept His simple answer. And that was what I did and He took care of it. It was a powerful lesson for me.

I am so envious of people who accept things on faith. Don't get me wrong, I'm not placing myself in the ranks of the highly educated intellectuals when I say that. My problem is a tendency to take the simplest concept, such as *"Be careful for nothing"* (Philippians 4:6) and analyze it and complicate it beyond recognition. My desire and my goal is to question those things which are *not* of God and deserve my scrutiny, and to accept those things which *are* of God without needing reason or proof. I'm getting closer, but I certainly haven't made it yet.

When I begin to get too analytical, I just remember that my life since entering recovery is proof enough for me of God's awesome power.

*He who is faithful in that which is least is faithful also
in much...*
Luke 16:10

I'm going through one of those "God is working with
me" periods. It's not unpleasant, simply uncomfortable and,
I might as well admit it, a little scary. Up to this point, my
idea of serving God, though sincere, always placed me in the
spotlight. I would envision my prison publication going to
every inmate in every prison. The magazines would be clam-
oring for my insightful articles. I would always have at least
one book on the best seller list. I would be in such demand as
a speaker that I could choose only the best locations for my
presentations. And so my fantasy went.

There's nothing wrong with dreams. We all need them.
However, when we allow those dreams to fill us with illu-
sions of grandeur, and we replace the One who gave us
the dream in the first place with pride and self—well, then
we have a problem. I had reached a place of declining any
opportunities that would not put a microphone in my hand or
spotlight my writing abilities. This was about the time God
began to deal with me.

We have a lady in our church that began to pervade my
thoughts. One day, as our Tuesday morning Bible study group
was preparing to begin, she walked through the fellowship
hall to the kitchen. We were all dressed in our nice casual
clothes, waiting to be spoon-fed the word of God. Her hair
was somewhat awry, she had on grubbies, and on her hands
were yellow rubber gloves. She was cleaning the church. I
mean really cleaning—bleach, scouring pads, etc.

I realized as I thought about this remarkable woman, that
I had never seen her with a microphone in her hand. But I had
often seen her with a vacuum cleaner, or her arms around a
sobbing parishioner, or hand in hand with one of the 6-year-
olds in her class as she leads him to the Lord, or kneeling in

prayer at the alter with a hurting friend, or cleaning the house of a sick acquaintance.

This is the type person I *know* God is calling me to be. It wasn't easy for me to take my eyes off my own vision and switch it to His. I have to admit it took me some time to surrender, but I have done it and now look for opportunities to serve Him in whatever capacity He desires.

I know this doesn't mean I will never have that best seller, for I may one day. But somehow, it's no longer of prime importance to me. My vision today is to be faithful even in–no, *especially in*, the little things.

*Confess your faults one to another, and pray one for
another, that ye may be healed. The effectual fervent
prayer of a righteous man availeth much.*
James 5:16

The Bible tells us that each believer is given a spiritual
gift (1 Cor. 12:11) to be used for the good of the whole. I've
come to believe that my gift is the desire to blurt out all
my faults, shortcomings, and out and out sins to the whole
world. This is done in hopes that others will either 1) see
the mistakes in me and avoid the pitfalls themselves, or 2)
see the same problem in their own lives and, realizing they
are not alone, start to do what needs to be done to correct it.
Having said that, here is my latest admission.

I do not understand praying for other people. I'm not
talking about family or friends, that I understand and do.
What I mean are the prayer requests coming from someone
I don't know very well for someone else that I know even
less or not at all. How can I possibly pray an effective prayer
for someone I've never even seen? And yet, there have been
times when I have done just that.

Recently a lady from my Sunday School class called me.
She said a friend of hers had a nephew somewhere that was
dying from pneumonia and her friend asked her to pray for
him. She said as she was preparing to pray for the young
man, God laid it on her heart to call me to pray for him. I did
not know my classmate's friend, nor did I know her son. But
I prayed fervently. I was afraid not to. And I continued to
pray until the young man died a couple of weeks later. Some
will say, "Well, that sure didn't do any good." I don't agree.
Yes, he did die, but who knows what all was accomplished
because of the prayers of family and friends and yes, even
strangers. God commands us to pray. Nowhere does it say
He is obligated to reveal to us the results of those prayers.

In the past, I have felt guilty concerning the people I don't pray for. I believe this is one of Satan's attacks. There are some for which we know we are to pray, our family, our pastors, our government leaders, and the lost. But beyond that I'm learning to trust God to bring to my mind those He wants me to pray for. I'm finding when I stay sensitive to His promptings and am obedient to follow them, I can pray sincere, fervent prayers. It doesn't always make sense to me, like praying for the man sitting in front of us at a movie, but I've learned that following God *won't* always make sense to me.

I'm getting excited about my prayer life since I've begun to look to God for guidance instead of seeking advice from the "prayer experts."

For God has not given us the spirit of fear, but of
power, and of love, and of discipline.
2 Timothy 1:7

Jabez's prayer. Our pastor preached a sermon on Jabez's prayer last week. His best sermon ever some say. (It would have to be one of the few Sundays I've missed in the last several years, but I've ordered a tape of it.) There is a book out called "The Prayer of Jabez" by Bruce Wilkinson. It's my understanding the pastor challenged the congregation to get the book, read it, and begin to pray Jabez's prayer.

It was not the first time I've heard of the book so I ordered it. It's a small book that can be read in a few hours. As a matter of fact, I started it yesterday evening and, unable to sleep, got up and finished it at 3:00 this morning. It's challenging to say the least.

Jabez is mentioned only once in the Bible (1 Chronicles 4:10). Here is his prayer, "*Oh, that thou wouldest bless me indeed, and enlarge my coast, that thine hand might be with me, and that thou wouldest keep me from evil, that it might not grieve me.*"

Simple prayer, right? It's simple only at first glance. The book explains the boldness of it and what can be expected (based on countless personal testimonies) when it is prayed regularly and with sincerity.

I want to pray it but it frightens me because the "enlarge my coast" part has no fill in the blanks where I can describe my definition of "coast" and specify my own preferences. Nope. It leaves me wide open for whatever God wants me to do, for *His* definition of coast.

Strangely enough (yeah, right), after acknowledging my fears to God, I picked up my daily devotional book and today's devotion was entitled, "How to handle our fears." It reminded me of the above verse. Some Bible versions of this verse use the word timidity (God has not given us a spirit of timidity). Either works for me because timidity *is* my fear. Suppose God's idea of expanding my coast includes going out on the streets to witness to strangers? I don't do well in that kind of situation.

I want to pray Jabez's prayer. But I don't want to do it until I can go into it 100% committed to going wherever God leads me and doing whatever those "enlarged coasts" require. I pray for God to give me the courage to step out and make that commitment.

The above verse tells me that God has not given me a spirit of fear. Therefore, I know where the fear is coming from and that alone tells me it isn't real. I expect to be stepping out in faith with Jabez very soon.

But I have prayed for thee, that thy faith fail not...
Luke 22:32

I've always been an optimist, even in the face of the myriad challenges I've endured during the course of my life. My parents were alcoholics. I endured childhood sexual abuse. My family often lived in the car. I became an alcoholic myself. I was married to an immature man who drank too much and had no concept of fidelity (I'm still married to him, but he is not the same man). I had a child who began taking drugs at 11 years old. And these are just the highlights. Yet I was always optimistic, knowing there was a better way to live. Not only that, I believed it was possible for me to have that better life. It may have taken me 45 years, but I do have it now.

The daughter I mentioned who started on drugs at such a tender age is now in her 25th year of addiction and is serving her 4th prison term. But I know with absolute certainty that she is not only going to make it, but she is also going to do something incredible with her life. Pollyanna attitude? No, but definitely optimistic.

I believe that optimism and faith go hand in hand. To be a true optimist, there has to be a firm belief in God and His ability and willingness to divinely intervene on our behalf.

Some say pessimistic thinking prevents disappointment. According to this theory, if you are not expecting anything good, you won't be disappointed when nothing good comes. I say this thinking is exactly backwards. If nothing good is expected, nothing good happens. It's self-fulfilling prophecy. We attract what we think about. The most devout pessimist I ever encountered was a neighbor of ours. He always expected the worst from every person and every circumstance and, consequently, he was a miserable person.

Optimism is contagious, but pessimism is much more so. That is why we must be careful with whom we associate. For several years our youngest daughter dated a young man who was a card-carrying pessimist, which was the primary reason they parted ways. She is a natural optimist, but instead of her positively affecting him, he was dragging her down to his level of negative thinking.

Those of us who walk with Jesus have every reason to be optimistic. There will be trials and tribulations as long as we live on this earth, but this is not our real home. We are only sojourners here. Our real home is waiting for us on the other side of this life and it will be perfect. What better reason to be optimistic?

*For God hath not given us the spirit of fear; but of
power, and of love, and of a sound mind.*
2 Timothy 1:7

My husband and I are on our way to our daughter's parole
hearing. If the board grants her parole, she will be released in
about four months. If they don't grant it, she will not receive
another hearing for twenty-one months. Because the board
uses a point system as the guideline for their decisions, and
because of the number of points her past record assigns her,
the odds are not in her favor. As the miles and the minutes
melt away on this early morning trip, my mind wants to
scramble here and there in fear. My thoughts have tried to
get away from me all week. With much prayer and help from
God, however, I have managed to keep the demons at bay.

Contrary to popular belief, the opposite of fear is not
courage it's faith. What difference does faith make? Well,
fear tells me that if she doesn't make parole this hearing,
she will be locked up for two more years. Fear tells me she
can't handle that and it will be too difficult for the rest of us.
Fear tells me it just *has* to be now. When we base our hopes,
dreams, plans, and feelings on a single outcome of an event,
we're setting ourselves up for disappointment, pain, anger,
and ultimately, failure.

Faith tells me that God, not the Board of Paroles, is in
control. Faith tells me if God is ready for her to be released,
all the points in the world are not going to make any difference. Faith tells me if God is not ready for her to be released,
she *will* be able to handle it, as will the rest of us. Faith tells
me I have nothing to fear. So in absolute faith, without any
fear, here is my prayer for this day:

Dear God, You know that the mother in me wants to pray
for our daughter's release. But experience has shown me that
what I think I want is not always best for those I love. I know
that as much as we love our daughter, You love her more.

Whereas we only see what's in front of us, You see the big picture. So, more than what I want, I pray for Your will in her life. If You're ready for her to be out, please open the hearts and minds of the commissioners and let her find favor with them. If she's not yet received all You have for her from this incarceration, let their decision reflect her need. You promise to work all things together for the good of those who love You. She loves You and I claim this promise for her. We accept Your will in this with absolute faith and an absence of fear. Amen.

Only faith allows me the peace and serenity to pray this.

*For as the body without the spirit is dead, so faith
without works is dead also.*
James 2:26

My church recently asked me to serve on the Stewardship
Committee which oversees all the expenditures and budgets
of the various departments. Evidently I had opened my
mouth in front of the wrong person, revealing my accounting
background.

My initial reaction was varied. I was, of course, flattered,
but that passed quickly. I thought I had left the accounting
behind me. I no longer do numbers. Then I thought, *I'm
already doing my share. I teach a Sunday morning Bible
Study, am responsible for putting together the monthly newsletter, attend and co-teach the Tuesday morning lady's Bible
Study, tithe, and speak before groups when asked. All of this
and it is a 150-mile round trip from our home to the church.*
I was doing that "pat myself on the back" thing while justi-
fying my desire to decline the request.

God wasn't buying any of it—neither the smugness
in what I was already contributing nor the excuses for not
serving on the committee. He reminded me that He was the
one who gave me the natural ability to work with numbers,
and just because I'm through with that type of work doesn't
mean He's through with using me for it. And after all,
shouldn't that 35 years of experience come to some good for
His kingdom?

Then came the chastisement for thinking I was already
doing my share. I've discovered that the principles that are
in operation in the work world also apply to the church,
and this includes the 80/20 rule. 80% of the work is done
by 20% of the people. It doesn't seem fair, but fair or not,
it's a fact. I've always been a member of that 20% in my
jobs, but never before in the church until now. Instead of
complaining, I realize how fortunate I am to be a part of the

20%. It has been my observation that the other 80% are the unhappy, disgruntled, complaining group. I want no part of that group.

Every church I attended before this one would find me walking in, sitting down, and saying, "Okay, give me something that will make me feel good this next week." Then I would leave. I never gave any thought to the work, effort, faith, and love that went into a church that is truly dedicated to loving others and displaying Christ to the world. Attending church and enjoying the fellowship is wonderful. We need it. God commands it. It is an awesome privilege that we should never take for granted, but with that privilege comes responsibility. We can't take and take and take without giving back. James says faith without works is dead. Our churches need our works.

Trust in the Lord with all thine heart; and lean not unto thine own understanding. In all thy ways acknowledge Him, and He shall direct thy paths.
Proverbs 3:5-6

This was my mother's favorite verse from the Bible. She had it written on yellow stickies all over her house. She repeated it often, yet never accomplished it. She could not seem to let go and believe that God would take care of her. She had a stubborn, "I'll do it myself," streak a mile wide. She didn't believe in going to God with the things that she "should" be able to take care of herself.

Mother's preacher and his family lived next door to her. I remember her telling me one day on the phone that she had gone next door and found them praying over their broken washing machine. She thought that was ridiculous. I tried explaining to her that my Bible says we are to pray about everything. It doesn't say everything except broken washing machines. She said, "You don't pray over broken washing machines. You have them fixed or replaced." I asked her what the end result was. She said she bought them a new one because they didn't have the money. Which was, of course, the reason they were praying about it in the first place. She had no comment when I observed that their prayer was answered.

My mother has gone on to be with God and is finally free of the worry that tormented her entire life. However, I still feel sad whenever I realize that her life, while on earth, could have been so much more peaceful and joyful if she would have lived her favorite verse.

Because of my mother, I grew up believing that not to worry was shirking responsibility. If I didn't worry, I must not fully understand the gravity of whatever situation might be at hand. Or worse I didn't care. I don't blame my mother for this. That's the way she was and it wasn't much fun for her either. But it's been a struggle for me to overcome these ideas and to find some balance.

I am just now learning to truly trust God; to lean on Him instead of my own understanding. What has made this possible for me? I'm finally coming to the knowledge of His love for me. I know that in this lifetime I can never know the depths of that love, but just knowing that it's more than I *can* know is enough. Because of that love, I know that He will do only what's best for me, in spite of how the circumstances may appear.

I wish my mother could have learned to trust Him with all her heart. But because of her negative example, I'm able to see the sweet difference between what she had and what I have, proving once again that God *"causes all things to work together for the good"* (Romans 8:28).

*So then faith cometh by hearing and hearing by the
word of God...*
Romans 10:17

Such a simple little verse, but so chock full of meaning.
We are ordered throughout the Bible to have faith. We are
told we are sanctified by faith (Acts 26:18), justified by
faith (Romans 5:1), we walk by faith (2 Cor. 5:7), live by
faith (Gal. 2:20), are saved through faith (Eph 2:8), have joy
in faith (Phil 1:25), faith produces stability (Col. 2:5), are
sound in the faith (Titus 1:13), and Hebrews 11:6 tells us that
it is impossible to please God without faith. Evidently faith
is something that is within the reach of all, or God would
not have told us it's imperative to have it to please Him. He
never commands us to do something without equipping us
with the ability to do it. So why do so many people have
such a problem with faith.

I'm not sure, but I do have a theory. Faith is not tangible,
and our society has taught us to never trust anything we
can't see. The world tells us to "believe it when you see it."
However, like so many of God's principles, the concept of
faith requires exactly the opposite attitude of the world and
that is, "you'll see it *when* you believe it." This very idea
is conveyed in God's definition of Faith in Hebrews 11:1,
*"Now faith is the substance of things hoped for, the evidence
of things not seen." "...evidence of things not seen,"* suggests
bringing into reality those things I believe but don't see. Still
people don't believe in faith. I've heard people say (some
from my own family), "If you can't prove it to me with
pencil and paper, don't even talk to me about it." What a sad
way to live.

God commands us throughout the Bible to have faith in
Him, but where does this faith come from? How do we get it?
Does He just open us up and pour it in and say, "Okay, that's
your measure of faith use it wisely?" Sometimes I think that

would be a pretty good way to go about it, but no, that's not how it happens. There would be no need to command us to attain something that He's going to give us anyway. So what is the deal here and how does it work?

God does give everyone a certain amount of faith, *"...as God hath dealt every man the measure of faith,"* (Romans 12:3). How much is a measure? I haven't a clue, but I do know that it is exactly the right amount for each person. So why can't we live perfect lives, walking in perfect faith? Because the "measure" given us is just seed faith, just a portion to bring us to Jesus and get us started. Then what? Well, then we step up to the plate and start exercising our responsibility in the process. And that involves reading His Word, which the beginning verse tells us is the method for growing faith. But just reading and hearing will not do it. We must act on what we read and hear, and go forward with it, and soon we will be mighty men of faith like those high-lighted in Hebrews 11.

Stone #9

Truth

❧

Lead me in thy truth, and teach me: for thou art the God of my salvation; on thee do I wait all the day.
Psalm 25:5

...and the truth of the Lord endureth for ever.
Psalm 117:2

Jesus said, "The truth will make you free," (John 8:32).
Garfield (the cat) said, "The truth will make you free, but first it will make you miserable." They are both right. I just received an e-mail from my niece who has been estranged from her father (my brother) for about 12 years. She off-handedly asked me if I thought her dad would want to talk to her. She said she could take the truth. Would he want to see her? The answer is I don't know but there is a possibility that he wouldn't. Could she take this answer? Yes, but on some level it would have to hurt. Do I want to tell her this truth? Absolutely not. So I will probably evade the question until and unless she brings it up again in which case I will face it. However, she is a smart lady and she will probably realize that my avoidance is, in itself, her answer.

Philosopher and poet George Santayana said, "The truth is cruel, but it can be loved and it makes free those who have loved it." As my little discourse proves, he is right, the truth can be cruel. Those truths, the cruel ones, are the ones I attempt to avoid either receiving or delivering. That is the coward's way out. While I don't believe we should just blurt out deliberately cruel truths, some cruel truths need to be faced and dealt with.

I always know when our daughter has relapsed and is back into the drug scene. This is one of those cruel truths I will go to any length to evade. But no matter what measures I employ, from arguing adamantly in her defense to burying my head in the sand, deep down I always know the truth. It's a strange thing about this kind of truth. Once I face it head-on and voice it to someone else, it loses much of its power to instill fear and hopelessness. This obviously (so obviously, I never realized it until this moment) is what Jesus meant when He said, "The truth will make you free." A truth faced, even a truly ugly one, is indeed a liberating experience.

People don't want to face certain truths because of fear. They are afraid the truth, the real truth, will change their realities. But as English writer Aldous Huxley said, "Facts do not cease to exist because they are ignored."

...remember not the sins of my youth, nor my
transgressions...
Psalm 25:7

While staying with our 13-year-old grandson, my husband and I took the opportunity on a Sunday morning to witness to him, who, to date, has not accepted Jesus. We started with a discussion about the conscience and how God uses it to draw us to Him.

As an illustration of the conscience, I relayed a story to him from my youth. When I was about 12-years-old, a friend and I stole costume jewelry, hair ribbons, makeup, etc. from a five-and-dime store (remember those before the Wal Marts, K Marts, and Targets?). Not knowing what to do with the "loot", I hid it under the house. My dad found it and confronted me with his discovery. I compounded my sin, which was already weighing heavy on my heart, by lying. Of course, I fooled no one, least of all my dad, but he let it drop.

So overcome with guilt and remorse, I was unable to sleep, or anything else for that matter. Finally one night, not wanting to endure the torment any longer, I stole into my parent's bedroom and woke them. Sobbing almost uncontrollably, I bared my soul and told them the truth. Ah the sweet release of confession. I felt cleansed and brand new. We tried explaining to our grandson that this is what happens when we invite Jesus into our hearts. He cleans up all the junk and makes us into a new person.

That was all of my youth I chose to tell him. I wish that account of my sin and subsequent conscience at age 12 was the last of my errant ways. Unfortunately, it was only the beginning. A person would think it was, at least, the last time I stole anything. Not so. Actually, I became quite adept at it. The conscience still kicked in, but I soon discovered that alcohol would soothe that savage beast. Of course, the alcohol also opened the door to a myriad of new problems. But it took me over 30 years to finally make the association between drinking and those problems.

I'm not proud of my youth and frequently regret the problems I caused my parents. The things I did must have caused them untold grief and broken their hearts. I also robbed myself of the joy of a carefree productive youth. The damage can never be undone and the lost years cannot be regained, but I can ask God to help me use them with actions such as witnessing to our grandson.

...and we were in our own sight as grasshoppers, so we
were in their sight.
Numbers 13:33

My favorite Bible teacher has a program on TV at 5:30 each morning. I watch her as I do my floor and weight exercises to help take my mind off the pain and monotony. She made an interesting statement one morning that made me think of this verse in Numbers. She said, We teach by what we allow." Don't see the connection between her comment and the verse? You will.

Moses sent twelve spies into Canaan to see what they would be facing when they entered into the Promised Land; whether the people who inhabited it were weak or strong, how many there were, etc. They all came back with the same facts. However, only two, Joshua and Caleb, had the faith that the Israelites could overtake the land and claim it for their own. The other ten were afraid of the enemy's numbers and size and gave an "evil report" (verse 32), believing they would be unable to conquer the Canaanites (even though God had already promised them the land).

All victory, or defeat, begins in the mind. The ten spies who gave the evil report were defeated before the battle ever began because in their minds they were convinced they could not win. We teach others how to treat us by how we feel about ourselves.

My own life is a classic example of this truth. Back in our drinking days, my husband was seldom home. He spent most of his free time in the bars drinking and enjoying the camaraderie of others who had equally empty lives. For years (many, many years) I felt that my low self-esteem and lack of self-confidence was because of the way he treated me. After all, if I were prettier, smarter, sweeter, etc., wouldn't he be home with me? I realize now that I had it backwards. He treated me the way he did because I didn't have any self-esteem and self-confidence. I didn't think I was good enough for anything better than I was getting, and consequently, I taught him to treat me in such a manner by not expecting or demanding anything more.

When I went into recovery and began to learn I was a child of God and deserved to be treated as such, things began to change. As I began to set boundaries concerning what I would and would not accept, he treated me accordingly. Truly we do teach by what we allow.

Need to remember this.!

...this is the work of God, that ye believe on him whom
he hath sent.
John 6:29

I am a doer. I want to do, to accomplish, to progress, to measure. Give me a goal I can get behind and get passionate about, or show me a plan and set me a deadline and I'm off and running, usually before the starting bell has even rung.

I don't believe I'm much different from others, and obviously we've not changed in the last 2000 years. It was the disciples questioning Him that prompted the above answer from Jesus. Verse 28 says, *"Then said they unto him, what shall we do, that we might work the works of God?"* They wanted to get about the business of God and wanted to know what they could "do."

Aren't we the same way? Most of us initially came to God broken, knowing that on our own we haven't a chance to do anything with our lives and, with childlike faith and trust, we turn it all over to Him. But then, sometimes before we even get off our knees, we're devising a plan for what we can do for God. "I know, I'll teach a Sunday School class." Or, "I will volunteer over here, and over here, and over here."

I'm not saying these things are bad. After all, James did tell us in James 2:17 that faith without works is dead. The problem lies not in our actions, but the motives behind our actions. We believe we can buy God's favor, and thus His blessings and peace for ourselves, through our good works. And we set about making our own plans and decisions about what God wants from us and we get busy "doing" to make it happen.

But notice Jesus' answer to the disciples, *"This is the work of God, that ye believe..."* He said work, singular, not works. All He wants from us is to believe. "It can't be that simple! You just got through telling me that faith without works is dead. I must have to do something more than just believe!" I hear your cries of protest. Been there, said that.

Follow through with me on this and you'll understand where it leads. If I start my walk simply believing, that belief is going to lead me into God's Word. I'm going to learn more and more of Him and His ways. I'm going to open up to the guidance and direction of the Holy Spirit. As I read and allow Him to work in my thoughts and my life, I will develop a desire to do only what He wants me to do. When that happens, He will begin to open doors of opportunity for me in the areas where He wants my works performed. So it's not what works I can do for Him, but what I am going to allow Him to work through me.

Blessed are the meek: for they shall inherit the earth.
Matthew 5:5

Some versions of the Bible have the word gentle instead of meek in this verse. The *Random House Dictionary* defines meek as "humbly patient, as when under provocation." The *Vines Greek Bible Dictionary* tells us that meek means "gentle and humble." So we see that the words meek and gentle are practically interchangeable.

However, in our macho competitive society of today, the word meek conjures up the vision of a weak-willed coward who's afraid of his own shadow. Unfortunately, the word gentle doesn't exactly invoke pictures of those who would be in charge of the world either. And yet, that is exactly what God is telling us in this verse. I can only surmise that our modern day concept of meek and gentle must be totally off the mark.

Let's look at Jesus who is to be our example in victorious living. On the day of His crucifixion He was beaten, taunted, spat upon, and ridiculed. Yet the Bible tells us, *"as a lamb to the slaughter, and as a sheep before her shearers is dumb, So He openeth not His mouth"* (Isaiah 53:7). Is there anyone who would call Jesus a coward? I think not. Earlier in His ministry, with whip in hand and rage filling His body with adrenaline, He overturned the tables of the moneychangers and run them from the temple (John 2:15). Hardly the act of a mild-mannered Clark Kent.

So why did He make that walk to Calvary like a lamb being led to slaughter? He could have called down a legion of angels to free Him if He desired. The answer is simple. He had a job to do and He was totally focused on doing it. He knew who He was in God and He was secure in His identity. He felt no need to prove Himself or to justify Himself. It wasn't important to Him what the crowd thought of Him or if they ridiculed Him with their taunts, such as, "If you're really the Son of God, let's see You get Yourself out of this mess." How many of us with His abilities would have been tempted to do just that and in a spectacular way? But Jesus had a mission to accomplish, and it didn't include a big show of power for the crowds.

Meek and gentle does not mean weak and cowardly. It takes a strong person, one who is sure of himself, one who knows who he is in Christ, to be gentle and meek. These are the people who God says will inherit the earth. I want to stand in that group.

> *Will a man rob God? Yet ye have robbed me. But*
> *ye say, Wherein have we robbed thee? In tithes and*
> *offerings.*
> Malachi 3:8

Yesterday I attended my first meeting as a member of our church's stewardship committee. It was an enlightening experience. I heard some appalling statistics. For instance, the average Southern Baptist church member gives $17 a week to his church. $17! That would be the tithe from $170. If that were the true salary of the average Southern Baptist, we would all be living well below poverty level (have you seen some of the cars these people drive?). Even worse than this number, I hear that the average church member in our church gives only $10 a week. This made me sad. It took a great deal of effort on my part not to cry (I didn't want them to wonder what kind of emotional kook they had voted in to their committee).

I consider our church exceptional. The people are warm and caring. They have a great love for God and a strong faith in the power of prayer. Our pastor is a great hulk of a man who openly weeps when he talks of the lost in the world. His sermons are stirring and thought provoking. Our membership is growing and we are building a new sanctuary. But unless something changes we will never worship in the new sanctuary. There are no funds to pay for it. People say, "If it's God's will, He'll provide for it." But God provides for His people *through His people*. If He has laid it on our hearts and commanded us to tithe, and He has, where do we think the provision will come from if we don't follow that command? It's the tragedy of the masses. Everyone thinks someone else will do it.

It's wonderful to go in to church on Sunday morning, get lots of hugs, sing a few songs, let the pastor say a few words that will make us feel good, drop a $5 bill in the plate and go home feeling very smug and superior. Why should I worry about how the electric bill gets paid, or whether or not the pastor has an insurance plan, or where the materials come from for the kid's Vacation Bible School? There are always people around who like to get involved—let them worry about it.

Peter Marshall, pastor and chaplain to the U. S. Senate, once said, "People should give in proportion to their income lest God make the incomes in proportion to the giving." Not a bad idea. We have an obligation to God. He tells us we are to spread His word. There are those who think talking about money is crass and unspiritual. Well, I'm sorry. I wish it weren't so, but money is necessary to get the word out.

James 1:17 says that every good thing given and every perfect gift comes from above. It's all His anyway. Why not throw back a tenth into the pot to further His kingdom?

*...no man having put his hand to the plough, and
looking back is fit for the kingdom of God.*
Luke 9:62

This is an interesting statement made by Jesus. What did
He mean? Looking at it in context, He said it to a man who
wanted to follow Him but first wanted to say goodbye to
his family. Jesus' answer to him may seem a little harsh to
us. However, I believe the message He wanted to convey to
the man, and to us as well, is that once we have made the
decision to follow Jesus, we mustn't look back at our past
and bring that baggage with us. The footnote in my Bible
for this verse tells me, "looking back will make the furrow
crooked." We can't bring "stuff" from a past *without* Jesus
into a future *with* Jesus.

My Bible Study teacher made a comment during a
recent class that gave me cause for thought. She said, "I
don't like talking about my past," and backed her statement
with Philippians 3:13, *"this one thing I do; forgetting those
things which are behind and reaching forth unto those things
which are before.."* I thought about how much I talk about
my past. Oh, not in regular conversation with others, but in
my teaching, my oral presentations, and my writing.

At first I was condemned by her statement, thinking I
was wrong in discussing my past so frequently (remember
I'm the one who constantly deals with guilt issues). But on
reflection, I realized it is okay, that it is actually an integral
part of my ministry.

My past is the very link I have with those to whom I
speak and for whom I write: the prisoners, the addicted, the
homeless, the hurting. Because of my past, I feel compassion towards them. I can relate to them. I can understand the
struggles they endure and the hopelessness that surrounds
them. And, in order for them to want to listen to me, they
must know I can relate to them. The only way relating to them

can be accomplished is to tell them, openly and honestly, my own story. It's effective and gets their attention.

My past is not pretty. I'm certainly not proud of it. But hiding it will not make it go away, so why not use it for the Lord? After all, He allowed me to live it, pulled me out of it, then gave me a desire to help others with it, and a talent to accomplish that desire. I realize not everyone is called to blurt out all their uglies in public. I guess I'm just one of the lucky (?) ones.

*So he called every one of his lord's debtors unto him,
and said unto the first, "How much owest thou unto my
lord?"*
Luke 16:5

How many of us actually consider that we owe a debt to
God? Don't we usually come to Him each morning (if we're
even into regular praying) with a long list of things He just
has to do to keep us happy that day?

Our oldest daughter, who is in prison, called yesterday
morning and said she had a difficult week—good but difficult. Apparently God has placed one of her roommates with
her to teach her a number of lessons, not the least of which
is patience (He does that kind of thing, you know). She said
through watching this girl, God has allowed her to see how
she herself has always been in her relationship with God.

She went on to explain that in the past she has always
gotten herself into messes, prayed for God to get her out,
and when He did, she took back control and resumed her
life as always, never giving a thought to her indebtedness
to God. She says the young lady talks about God, reads her
Bible, professes to pray, but there is no spiritual manifestation in her life. She has no compassion for others, no love,
and makes no attempt to reach out. In other words, there is
no walk to match her talk.

Our daughter was not telling me these things in a judg-
mental or critical way. On the contrary, she was filled with
sadness and humility. She saw herself using other people for
her benefit and, even worse, using God. As I said, the revelation was difficult for her, but good. She said she wants only
to spend the rest of her life in a manner that will be pleasing
to God, giving to Him instead of taking from Him.

God gave us an awesome gift when He sent His Son to
earth. We have but to believe in Him and we are promised
eternal life in heaven with Him. We cannot even imagine

how wonderful that will be. The gift is free and the eternity with Him is assured. However, we have a responsibility to Him, there is an obligation, a debt we owe. Do we have to pay it? No, as I said, the gift of eternal life is free. But I can assure you that until you take your responsibility seriously and begin to live in a God-centered way, there will be no joy and no peace in *this* life.

We cannot take and take and take without ever giving back. When God gives to us with such love and compassion and generosity, He wants us to repay Him by passing it on to others, and not just those *we* deem worthy, but to everyone.

Said I not unto thee, that if thou wouldest believe, thou
shouldest see the glory of God?
John 11:40

Jesus spoke this to Martha as He was about to raise her brother, Lazarus, from the dead. Martha felt Jesus had tarried so long getting there that it was too late for Him to do anything.

We may say, "Well, that's crazy. If I had been with Jesus and seen the miracles He performed, I wouldn't have doubted His ability to do anything." Oh, really. We may not have seen the miracles with our own eyes, but we have the inspired written accounts of those who did. And what about the miracles that God has performed in our own lives? Even with all of this first and second-hand knowledge of His miracles, how often are we convinced there is no way even Jesus could straighten out the messes in which we are mired?

We, as Christians, like to call ourselves believers, but just how much *do* we believe and how strong is that belief? We are a society of doers. The more activity the better. The more notches on the belt signifying accomplishments, the better we feel about ourselves. The size of our bank account, the kind of car we drive, and the neighborhood in which we live is how we measure our self-worth.

Comparison to others, both favorably and unfavorably, is a national pastime. Tangible things such as money, position, trophies, awards, cars, promotions, and possessions are easy to measure and keeping score is a snap. Belief? Where does that fit in? You can't put it in the bank. You can't drive it. You can't put a number on it. You can't tell by looking if you have more or less than the next person. So what good is it in this highly competitive, dog-eat-dog world?

It will save your life. It will bring you to an understanding that all the "things" of the world, while nice to have, are fleeting—here today and gone tomorrow. They bring no peace and there is no happiness in them. Once a level is attained in the world, you are driven to go, do, be, and accomplish the next level. And you must never let down your guard because there is always someone right at your heals ready to overtake you. It's not called a "rat race" for nothing.

Only believe. That's all God is calling us to do. If we just get to that point, then the other parts of our lives "magically" fall into place. Matthew 6:33 tells us "...*seek ye first the kingdom of God, and His righteousness; and all these things shall be added unto you.*" We don't have to get out there and scramble and compete and live in stress and turmoil. We have only to believe and God will take care of the rest.

And they entered in, and found not the body of the Lord
Jesus.
Luke 24:3

Today is Easter. (Easter is a strange word. I must
remember to look up the origin of it.) The day is set at a
strange time also. Unlike Christmas, which is always on the
25th of December, or Thanksgiving which is always the 4th
Thursday in November, the day we recognize as Easter is
dependent on moon phases. It's not even always in the same
month. Though usually in April, it is occasionally in March.
However, the actual day we recognize is not the issue. What
is vital is what it commemorates—the most important event
in the history of the world.

Easter is the day we celebrate the resurrection of Jesus
Christ; the day God raised Him from the dead. It was the
beginning of God's Covenant of Grace. No longer would
man be required to practice endless rituals in an attempt to
please God. No longer would we be required to depend on a
priest to make sacrifices to atone for our sins. God Himself
had provided the ultimate sacrifice, opening the door for man
to enter His very presence through the simple belief in this
Sacrifice. God declared the precious blood that was shed on
the cross sufficient to wash clean the sins of the entire world:
past, present, and future.

As I was mentally preparing for my Sunday School class
this morning, I decided we will read the story of the resurrection from one of the Gospels. In addition, I will ask for
a couple of testimonies on "What the resurrection means to
me personally." One of the many things I have learned from
my husband is to never ask anyone to do something I'm not
willing to do myself. So I started thinking about what my
testimony would be in this regard.

Our pastor once asked the question, "Did you know that
if you were the only sinful person who had ever lived, Jesus

would have died just for you—just to cleanse your sins?." This brought the crucifixion and the resurrection pretty close to home. The Easter story was no longer just an interesting tale to listen to once a year. It had become personal. It had become real.

Easter is a story of love. Not just any love, though. Not love as we know it. Not love as we experience for each other. But love that is willing to suffer the agony of a slow and painful death. Love that readily entered the very depths of hell to pay for my sins. My sins. Unbelievable love. How sad it is that the majority of people reject this most perfect gift of love.

Faithful is he that calleth you, who also will do it.
1 Thessalonians 5:24

What an incredible verse. First of all, God calls us to something. Then He turns around and makes it happen. I don't know how He does it, but my life is a testimony to the fact that He does.

Several years ago God allowed me to hit bottom in my alcoholic journey. I had come to a dead end. There were no turns in the road, and continuing forward was not an option. He was calling me to a life of sobriety, and reaching up for His hand was the only choice I had. Unless, of course, I just ended it all. I must admit I seriously considered that route several times, but I knew that wasn't what I really wanted. I was scared. I didn't know how *not* to drink. I had to totally depend on Him to show me, one day at a time (ever notice how He allows us to work our way into those totally dependent situations?). And show me He did. He called me into a life of glorious sobriety and then taught me how to live it.

He also called me to give up all attempts at controlling my family. He showed me that any sense of control I thought I had was only an illusion anyway. I was scared again. After all, what would happen to them if I wasn't constantly right on top of everything? It wasn't easy and it didn't happen overnight, but slowly I began to release my hold. I quit cleaning up their messes and allowed them to suffer the consequences of their actions. It hurt. It hurt me and it hurt them. More than once I screamed at God, "See, they *can't* make it! They *have* to have me!"

The only answer I ever received in one of those fits was, "Trust Me." So I did and slowly they started to become real people, full of abilities, talents, compassion, and a respect for me I had never allowed them to experience. He called me to turn loose of them, then He accomplished, in short order, what I had been trying to do in all their lives.

He called me out of an accounting career into a writing career at the age of 52. I knew nothing about writing except I loved to do it and seemed to have some natural talent for it. But when I stepped out, things began to happen. The right people showed up. Ideas came to me. Circumstances fell into place. He called me to write and He gave me the words and the audiences.

God is constantly trying to bring us out. From bad habits, from poor acquaintances. From shoddy living. From tacky words. But He never takes us out and leaves us hanging. Deuteronomy 6:23 says, *"And he brought us out from thence, that he might bring us in..."* He's right there to lead us into a new, better, more joyful way of life. Let Him call you then let Him accomplish it.

...which is the first commandment of all...thou shalt love the Lord thy God with all thy heart, and with all thy soul, and with all thy mind, and with all thy strength...
Mark 12:28,30

Last week my husband and I went camping, which is my favorite recreational pastime. One morning, as we were fishing, I was reflecting on the beauty of the lake and the surrounding mountains (and there was plenty of time for reflection since the fish weren't biting). I found myself asking God's forgiveness for not loving Him as I should. I then went on to ask forgiveness for my other sins. This brought one of those flashes of insights from God that I have come to treasure so much.

God showed me that not loving Him as I should, and not keeping my eyes and focus on Him *is* my sin. All the other sins stem from this one sin. Think about it. If I loved God with all my heart, soul, mind, and strength, would I be out in the world acting selfishly? Would I be engaging in gluttony, procrastination, pride, etc.? Would I be allowing a bad attitude, a sour mood, or a period of depression to ruin not only my days, but the days of all of those around me? I think not.

When we love God as Jesus commanded in this verse, we are always going to reflect the nature of God, which we know is love, light, goodness, and righteousness. When our love for God permeates every nook, corner, and crevice of our being, there is simply no room for the selfishness that breeds all other sin.

We know that we will never attain perfection in this lifetime. And yet, God commands us to love Him with our whole being and, if we do, we will eliminate all sin. This is a seeming contradiction. God never commands us to do something that is impossible, and yet, we know that the total love for Him that would bring perfection is impossible.

I've reconciled this seeming contradiction for myself by bringing in the understanding and experience I have concerning process. Perfect, all-encompassing love for God is not going to just happen. It is a process that takes place little by little, from glory to glory (2 Cor. 3:18). Then, when we meet Jesus upon our death or His return, whichever occurs first, what is left to be done of the process will be accomplished in the *"twinkling of an eye"* (1 Cor 15:52). Our responsibility is to work diligently in the process with God so that there will be very little left for Him to change in the end.

But lay up for yourselves treasures in heaven, where
neither moth nor rust doth corrupt...
Matthew 6:20

I am currently listening to a set of tapes entitled "The Seven Sacred Truths." To develop this audio program, the author interviewed hundreds of people over the age of 70, asking each one the following question, "What are the seven major lessons you have learned in your lifetime?." Though the subjects were scattered across the country and came from all walks of life, their answers were surprisingly uniform, and one of those answers reflects the truth of the above verse.

Nearly 100% of these "old timers" echoed God's message of the unimportance of material possessions. If we have not all come to this realization yet, and apparently we haven't judging by the success of the advertising business, we do know in our hearts that material things are temporary.

The beautiful white Cadillac I love today will probably be in a junkyard within ten or fifteen years. For sure it will be out of our lives since we already have plans to trade it. I have a few pieces of jewelry that mean a lot to me. Not because of their monetary value, but because my husband gave them to me as a token of love at a time in our lives when I desperately needed tangible assurance of his love for me. Though I cherish them, I no longer need them for that reason, and their importance is not in owning them.

I have sympathy for those who feel their main purpose in life is to acquire and accumulate. My sorrow arises from first-hand knowledge of the despair that motivates this frantic activity, which is doomed to failure. I spent many years of my life trying to fill that empty hole with people, places, and things. The more I tried, the emptier it became, and the more I drank. What a glorious day it was when I discovered that the hole was God-shaped and that He had been sitting quietly on the side lines, waiting to be invited to come in and fill it.

As the above verse indicates, we are not to waste our precious time on this earth accumulating more, more, more. (Contrary to popular belief, more is *not* better.) Yes, we have to work to support our families, but beyond supplying our needs, which God promises to do, our time and efforts are to be spent on kingdom treasures, and that will *always* involve helping others. Ironically, when we quit concentrating on ourselves and begin to focus on others, the blessings seem to chase us down.

For unto you is born this day in the city of David a
Saviour, which is Christ the Lord.
Luke 2:11

Christmas is my very favorite time of the year. I usually start talking about it around the middle of October, probably because that's when the holiday catalogs begin to arrive in the mail. (I do a lot of shopping by mail, so by Dec. 1, I'm getting an average of eight catalogs a day. I know the post office personnel love it.) My husband insists we wait at least until after Thanksgiving to start pulling out decorations and thinking about a tree. By that time my excitement is at a high pitch where it remains until the day after Christmas. Then I'm ready to take everything down and put it away for another year.

I don't remember very many Christmases when I was young which is probably just as well. There was one when I was 5 or 6, living in my great-grandmother's house, but the only thing I remember about that was my dad and I going out to chop down a tree. Then there was the one when my brother and I found all our toys and played with them before Christmas, which of course, ruined the whole day for us. I do remember our first Christmas in West Texas when I got my first bicycle. To this day I do not know how my mother got the money for it. On my last Christmas at home before I got married, my dad gave me a doll because I felt I had quit receiving dolls at too young an age. I wish I still had her.

About the first 15 Christmases after I got married were nightmares. We always went back to my parents for the holiday, and my husband would always go off with his friends and get drunk. I'm so grateful those days are over.

However, none of these memories, whether good or bad, are about the true meaning of Christmas—celebrating the birth of our Savior, Jesus Christ. He came to us as a newborn babe and went out 33 years later in a cloud of glory. The next time He comes to us will be as a King coming for His people to take them home. I can hardly wait.

It has taken me a long time to appreciate the true meaning of Christmas. It's definitely not about how much I can buy for my kids. I hope to be able to convey to them that our love for each other and Jesus are the most important things.

Behold, thou desirest truth in the inward parts, and in
the hidden part thou shalt make me to know wisdom.
Psalm 51:6

This verse is lifted from, in my opinion, the most beautiful of David's Psalms. It was written as he finally acknowledged his sin with Bathsheba and he had to go deep within himself to find the truth God desired from him.

I spent most of my life as a liar. (I just spent several agonizing minutes trying to find a softer gentler way of saying that. However, God seldom allows me to gloss over my sins with pretty words.) My lies were necessary to protect the image I felt I needed to project. I was sure no one would like me, much less love me, if they knew the real me—the ugly me that I worked so hard to keep hidden with my lies.

It was brought to my attention very early in recovery that the lies had to go. One of AA's powerful truths is that we're only as sick as our secrets. Getting past the lying was not an event, it was a process. We don't give up lifetime habits overnight. But through determination and conscious effort, the lies became fewer and further between. I was amazed in the beginning of this "clean up" effort how easily a lie rolled from my tongue. I had to be on my guard each time I opened my mouth. God stuck with me through the process and victory was finally gained. I'm grateful to say that today you couldn't pry a lie from my mouth on a bet.

Because of this, I was puzzled when I began to feel that God was dealing with me about honesty. I was living in an honest way, never lying. But it was not my words He was seeking to overhaul—it was my motives, the innermost being stuff. When I started looking in that area, I wasn't pleased with what I saw.

Yes, I was doing things to help others, but not because I had a great concern for their welfare. I did it because it made me feel good and because I thought it made me look good in the eyes of others. (I told you, God seldom let's me gloss over my uglies.) I was nice to people, not because I wanted to spread God's love, but because I wanted everyone to like me and say nice things about me. This had always been a pattern of mine. I had exchanged my lies for the truth of God but I wasn't using it as He intended.

Truth in the innermost being is not easy and can be very painful. However, we must allow God access to that place so that He can make us to know wisdom and set us free with His truth.

And God, which knoweth the hearts put no difference
between us and them...
Acts 15:8-9

I believe being in a minority is simply an issue of location and nothing more. Within the small town where I live,
my white skin places me in the majority and the two or three
black families who live here, in the minority. But suppose
those two or three black families and my white family were
magically picked up from this small town, swept away, and
set down in a village in the middle of Africa. How might that
change the designations?

I do not understand minority. We are each such unique
individuals — no two of us alike. I can only assume minority
doesn't mean different (since we *all* are), but maybe it
means *more* different. For instance, if I were in a room full
of blondes, my hair color would deem me a member of the
majority. (I prefer to call my hair platinum — never mind if
you prefer to call it silver, or even, bite your tongue, gray.)
This would be true even though no two people would have
exactly the same color, only different shades of blond. But
put me in a room full of brunettes and I suddenly become a
minority. Why are those labels important and what do they
mean?

They say (there's the illusive "they" again) that the
majority rules but I don't believe that. It's a wonderful idea
and I wish it were true, but I think that the"'silent majority"
better describes reality. Most people do not want to say or do
anything about anything as long as their lives are not being
directly affected. Apathy is the word that best describes the
masses.

I've always felt that God must love variety. Who would
think, of the 12 billion plus people who have existed since
the beginning of time, that He could make each one different
from all that came before and all that would come after. But

He did. So I repeat my question, how can there be minorities in a world full of people who are all different from each other?

A lot of the world's problems could be alleviated if people would start to look at the shared qualities we all have instead of focusing on the differences. We are all children of God, he loves us all, and He has commanded us to love each other. We don't do that. Or if we do, it's on a selective basis. We feel it's our right to pick and choose who we will love based on our own prejudices. We have no such right. God tells us to love one another. Period. No qualifiers.

He that believeth on the Son hath everlasting life.
John 3:36

I love philosophy: reading it, reading about it, studying it. It fascinates me the way some people's minds work. I believe I could have been a reasonably good philosopher had I started earlier and not spent over 30 years in a bottle. But since I did, I'm content to read, study, and listen to the great philosophers of our day and days gone by.

Everyone has a philosophy whether they realize it or not. Those who don't know they have one are more prone to having philosophies that change with the wind, but they still have one. Some are simple, such as Alice Roosevelt Longworth's, "I have a simple philosophy. Fill what's empty. Empty what's full. And scratch where it itches." Some are a bit more complicated, like that of Epictetus, one of the long ago philosophers who stated, "Here is the beginning of philosophy: a recognition of the conflicts between men, a search for their cause, a condemnation of mere opinion and the discovery of a standard of judgement."

My philosophy runs closer to Ms. Longworth's in simplicity than to Epictitus. I believe in God. I believe God created the world in six days, six 24-hour days, just like the Bible says. I believe that Jesus Christ is the Son of God. I believe He was born of a virgin. I believe He died on the cross for our sins. I believe He was resurrected from the grave. I believe He now sits at the right hand of God, and is coming back for His own. And I believe that all who believe these things will spend eternity in heaven. It follows that I believe in heaven, just as I believe in hell. I also believe that we're all going to be surprised at who is seen in both places.

I believe each person has that special place within that contains all the needed answers. I believe that we can learn how to draw out those answers once we develop a personal relationship with God and sensitivity to the Holy Spirit.

I believe integrity is the foundation on which a successful life is built. Until a person learns to make commitments and to keep those commitments (even if, and maybe especially if, they are only to himself), there can be no happiness and consequently, no success (at least, success according to Kay). It's been said that a man is only as good as his word, and I believe that.

Further beliefs: children are to be loved, nourished, protected, and hugged. Pets are to be loved and pampered. Husbands are to be loved, spoiled, and catered to. Mothers are to be cherished and fathers are to be revered. Strangers are to be given the benefit of the doubt and friends are to be given loyalty. And most importantly, God is to be given the number one place in our lives.

For I am the Lord, I change not.
Malachi 3:6

Nobel Prize-winning German poet and novelist, Hermann Hesse, said, "There is no reality except the one contained within us. That is why so many people live on such an unreal level. They take the images outside themselves for reality and never allow the world within to assert itself." I'm not at all sure I know what reality is. I know what it is for me today. But that may change tomorrow and it may be different from yesterday. And it may bear absolutely no resemblance to what another considers reality.

I once heard a quote (I believe from an ancient sage), "That is real which does not ever change." My spirit can bear witness with this definition. But what is it that does not change? The earth, stars, galaxies, and in fact, the whole universe, though set up in incredible synchronicity and order, are all very dynamic and constantly changing. People and, consequently, relationships change daily, if not hourly. Think that your current position with the company is a reality? Remember that thought tomorrow when you are standing in the unemployment line.

So, if by this definition none of these things can be our reality, what is? There is only one reality and that is God, as stated in the above verse. Hebrews 13:8 tells us that He is the same yesterday, today, and forever. And since we know that He has come to live within the born again believer, then within is where me must go for our reality, just as Mr. Hesse says.

I used to base my reality on my circumstances, relationships, and my current feelings, all of which were subject to drastic change at any moment. No wonder I drank so much for so many years! A person simply cannot define reality by what goes on around him and stay clean, sober, and sane.

Most things that are reality for me today are, ironically, intangibles. These are things that cannot be seen but are more real than the desk at which I sit. My reality originates from the center of my being where God resides. Reality is in the form of the values against which I try to measure all of my thoughts and actions. I must admit that there are times when I fall far short, but I try not to let those times be a source of discouragement.

At the top of my list of values is making my love relationship with God (which is a true reality for me) my number one priority. Next is truth and honesty in all my thoughts, words, and actions. Truth and honesty never change. If we buy into the current popular belief that truth and honesty are relative, well, we're only kidding ourselves. My other values include goodness, love, faithfulness, kindness, patience, etc. You know, all those fruits of the Spirit mentioned in Galatians 5:22-23. Now that's real reality.

He was oppressed, and He was afflicted, yet He opened
not His mouth
Isaiah 53:7

Why? Why did Jesus not open His mouth when He was being led to His death like a lamb to slaughter? I believe it was because there was nothing left to say. He had said it all. His ministry was over. It was time for Him to die.

How many of us keep on talking when there is nothing left to say? Jesus knew He was right and His executioners were wrong. When we know we are right, it is so difficult to keep our mouths shut. We want to keep hammering our point home until the other person comes to his senses and agrees with us. This describes me perfectly back in my drinking days. I would argue my case so vehemently and for so long that people would finally agree with me just to get me to shut up. I still have the tendency to want to do that. However, God is dealing with me about it and we are making progress.

There are people close to me, people whom I love dearly, who do not believe as I believe about a number of things (surprise, surprise). When disagreement occurs it disturbs me and my initial impulse is simply to stay away from people who disagree with me, and, in the past, I was fairly successful at doing just that. But I'm now coming to the conclusion, through God's promptings and revelations, that avoidance is not the solution. Oh sure, it keeps me nice and serene, but it doesn't give me opportunity to be a good witness to others. So God has been busy placing these people in my path.

When someone makes a comment such as, "Well yes, I believe Jesus was a real person and a good teacher, but the Son of God? I don't think so," the hair on the back of my neck stands up and I immediately become defensive. Not exactly an example of Christian demeanor. I saw this reaction often in my mother, and each time I feel it bubbling up in me, I have a vision of her being angry, flustered, and refusing to listen to the other side. This vision alone is often enough to calm me. My goal, however, is not to *get* calm, but to *stay* calm in these situations.

I notice Jesus never browbeat anyone with His truths. He stated them, shared them, and taught them to all who asked and wanted to hear. But He left it to God to open the minds and work in the hearts of those who heard. He knew there would be those who wouldn't listen or who would listen but not hear. These are the ones who broke His heart, but though He still loved them, He knew He couldn't force understanding onto them. Often, I too must not open my mouth, but simply let His light shine through me for others to see.

For I am in a strait betwixt two, having a desire to
depart and to be with Christ; which is far better.
Philippians 1:23

I have our daughter's name written beside this verse in my
Bible. The daughter who has a long running drug problem.
The daughter who spent several periods behind bars. The
daughter who has taught me so much about loving Jesus.

The first time I heard her say it, I was telling her about a
friend who had just died. "Oh, lucky him," was the response
that struck fear in my heart at the time. Similar comments
followed on various occasions. Though I never knew how
to respond, and therefore didn't, her statements always bothered me.

I knew it wasn't uncommon for older people, especially
those who are ill, to welcome death. Even my own grandmother, several months before she died, told me she was tired
and ready to move on to the next life. But she was 95-years-
old! I could understand that. My daughter was in her early
thirties when she began to make these comments. I worried.
Did she have a death wish? Was she suicidal? It certainly
was not unheard of among those who led her lifestyle. But
it just didn't seem to fit with the spiritual progress she had
made. I constantly worried, until God brought understanding
to me.

One day in Sunday School class, our teacher was talking
about another church member who was near death. Our
teacher made the offhanded comment as he was leaving
the subject, "I envy him." I kept him after class asking for
clarification of the comment, telling him of my daughter's
similar statements. He told me it was not a death wish at all.
It wasn't a desire to get away *from*, but a desire to go *to*.

My own spiritual growth slowly brought understanding.
Throughout Paul's letters to the New Testament churches, he
expressed a desire to move from this life (which, let's face

it, is full of pain, heartache, and tribulation) to the next life with Jesus. As I studied God's word, I began to experience the desire myself. It is impossible for the believer to read of Heaven, God's attributes, the things that await us, without looking forward to the time when we will actually be face to face with the reality of it all.

I feel sorry for those who fear death, and I believe there are only two groups of people who do: the unbelievers and the immature Christians. The solution to looking forward to the experience of death with gleeful anticipation is the same for both groups — get into the Word and see what awaits those who love God and are called according to His purpose.

...behold, I make all things new...
Revelations 21:5

Tomorrow is the first day 2001, the new millennium (in spite of all the hype last year as we entered the year 2000). I've decided I don't want to carry all of the baggage of my bad habits into the future. In the past I've stopped short of a total surrender to God—always keeping a few areas to myself—a few bad habits, a few worldly thoughts. I've come to realize that these are the very areas that cause me problems, so I'm now ready for that total surrender. As we journey into a new millennium, I eagerly look forward to an ever-deepening relationship with God. I don't know what total surrender will entail or what it will bring, but I'm no longer afraid of it.

I'm not making a lot of New Year's resolutions. Most of my goals consist of continuing with improvement programs already started in this year. I do, however, have two new ones. Number one is to finish this book. God put a desire in my heart to write a book several years ago. I've thought of it constantly which is a sure indication to me that it is from God. I've tossed back and forth various subjects, making several starts that currently lie in state, stored on disks in my bottom desk drawer. I now know that it was all preparation for this book. Hebrews 11:1 tells us that *"faith is the substance of things hoped for, the evidence of things not seen."* My faith is very strong in this area, though at this writing, the book has not yet been manifested into the physical world.

My other main resolution is to simplify my life, to quit analyzing everything. I have a habit of taking everything apart in an effort to understand the why and wherefore of it. When engaged in this habit, I leave myself wide open for the enemy to reduce my absolute wonder of God's creation and His workings to mere circumstance and happenstance. I want these things to be for me as they should—awesome miracles that keep me overflowing with gratitude. God has already provided me with an excellent example to follow in keeping this resolution—my husband. Though a relatively new Christian, his faith goes far beyond that of most of us who have professed belief for many years. If God said it in His Word, that's the end of it for my husband. No need to analyze it or wonder about it. If God performs a miracle in your life, thank Him and don't look for reasons why. If something bad happens, accept that He will work it together for the good and go on. Does this work? All I can tell you is that my husband is the most balanced, peaceful person I know, and my goal is to become that kind of person.

> *...but he that is greatest among you, let him be as the younger....*
> Luke 22:26

Charles Reade, English novelist and dramatist, said, "Not a day passes over the earth, but men and women of no note do great deeds, speak great words, and suffer noble sorrows." I suppose if you were to ask a dozen people what qualifies as a great person, you would probably get a dozen different answers. Some consider monetary success greatness. Actually, for many this is the primary criteria. For others it is power, though this often goes hand-in-hand with money. For still others it is professional or academic accomplishment. As I said, each person has his own definition.

So what is my opinion of greatness? A mother who takes her responsibility towards her family seriously. She is up early every morning cooking a real breakfast for her husband and children. She is organized and actively involved in her children's school and after-school curriculum. She does volunteer work and runs her home effectively and efficiently. The entire family attends church together and serves the church in various capacities. She takes good care of herself and assures she always has time for her own interests. Her relationship with God is her number one priority in life. Right behind Him is her family and they think she is wonderful. I realize this particular description of greatness may not be popular with the women-libbers out there, but it does fit in with the Proverbs 31 woman.

Other examples of greatness? As Charles Reade said in the opening quote, ordinary people doing great things such as signing an organ donor card, carrying a meal to a sick neighbor, helping an elderly person pump his gas at a self-serve station, babysitting so a young couple can have some time to themselves, visiting a convalescent center and reading to or writing letters for the patients. There are countless millions of common people out there doing great deeds. Their kindness, unselfishness, and greatness go unsung because they don't qualify as sensational. Too bad—they deserve recognition.

God, of course, is the greatest, and I can hardly wait until I meet *that* greatness face to face.

Shall their unbelief make the faith of God without effect?
Romans 3:3

Our youngest daughter called tonight. She was upset. She has a friend who is a professed atheist and our daughter had spent the afternoon talking to her about God, trying to get her to come to a place of belief. She was frustrated because she didn't feel she had made any progress.

Our daughter's friend is a very intelligent person, having graduated from law school. I've known a number of knowledgeable people who have difficulty accepting God. Why is that?

This friend told our daughter about a logic class she took in college. One of their assignments was to prove, using logic, that it is impossible for God to exist and they did it (where *do* we get these professors?). Logically speaking, it is *not* possible for God to exist. That is where faith enters the picture. We cannot search for God in the natural realm. John 4:24 tells us, *"God is a Spirit: and they that worship Him must worship Him in spirit and in truth."*

Many of the "super intellect" seem to have the attitude, *If I can't see it and/or prove it on paper, it doesn't exist.* God's plan is much too simple and basic for them. *"Whosoever believeth in Him, should not perish but have everlasting life"* (John 3:16). Just believe? Much too simple. Perhaps, though, attitudes are changing. I recently read that in the past if a scientist was asked if he believed in God, he would reply, "Of course not, I'm a scientist." Today that same scientist will answer, "Of course I believe in God, I'm a scientist."

There are far too many things in this universe for which God is the only answer. Each new major archeological discovery verifies the validity of the Bible. But God doesn't need science to validate Him. His truth is what it is. What I believe, what you believe, what the super genius believes, what the mentally challenged believes, none of it changes the truth. It's not God's will that any should perish, but He is not going to push His truths on us. He makes that truth available to us and reinforces it everywhere we look if we care to see it but it's our responsibility to receive it.

I understand our daughter's frustration. As believers we do not know why others cannot see the truth that is so plain to us. We pray for God to open the eyes of spiritual understanding for those who think they are too wise to see the truth. But believe or not, the truth of God will not change.

...that the power of Christ may rest upon me.
2 Corinthians 12:9

One night I made the trip to visit our oldest daughter who was, at the time, incarcerated in the county detention center (that sounds so much kinder than county jail). She made a comment to me that I was not able to get out of my mind. She said that even at the height (or would it be depth?) of her drug addiction, she had never felt so out of control of her life as she currently did. This made me realize some interesting things about control and power.

I believe what our daughter was really saying is that her circumstances were totally out of her control. And at that particular time she was correct. She had given over that control to the legal system when she chose to go against both her conscience and the laws of our land. However, I think that she was confusing her circumstances with her life, her essence, her self, who she is. That part of her is always under her power no matter what the circumstances. And that is true of each of us. You may ask how this can be, especially when I am specifically speaking of someone in jail.

Circumstances come and they go. They can change instantly, in the twinkling of an eye. Sometimes we can control them, but often they are out of our realm of influence. If we base our feelings of power and self-worth on what is going on around us, our lives and emotions will be as passengers on a roller coaster; reaching for the heavens one moment and plunging to the depths of hell the next.

Our real power, the God-given control in our lives, is revealed in how we choose to view our circumstances and then what action we take based on that observation. The choice is always ours. That's where the power comes in. Of course, we can choose to give away that power. This is what happens when we simply react off the top of our heads to what is going on around us instead of taking the time to analyze the situation and respond appropriately.

Power has nothing to do with a person's position in life. The president of the United States has no more power than I have. He has a lot more authority, but only I have power over my life unless I give it away. Never confuse power with authority and never confuse your circumstances with who you are.

Stone #10

Grace

Behold now, thy servant hath found grace in thy sight, and thou hast magnified thy mercy, which thou hast shewed unto me in saving my life...
Genesis 19:19

*Let us therefore come boldly unto the throne of grace,
that we may obtain mercy, and find grace to help in
time of need.*
Hebrews 4:16

The verse preceding this one tells me the reason I can go to the throne of grace with confidence. Not because of anything wonderful I've done. If that were the case, maybe I could timidly approach it today but tomorrow couldn't even entertain the thought. No, I can approach God with boldness and confidence because of Jesus and the work He did on my behalf.

The second part of this verse tells me three things. First, I am going to have times of need. Notice, it doesn't say *if* you have times of need. Second, it tells me that God's mercy and grace are what is required to get me through those times of need. And third, it tells me the mercy and grace are available to me. My responsibility is to receive them. It doesn't say I should go out and earn them with my good works. Or that I have to get down on my knees and beg God to give them to me. It says I am to receive them.

God gave me a beautiful revelation on grace one morning and I have been very grateful because it explained a lot of questions I occasionally had rolling around in my head. I was driving to Bible study and listening to a tape on grace by one of my favorite Bible teachers. I was thinking about the different circumstances, some extremely difficult, that people have to face. We've all seen people go through painful trials and wonder how they were able to do it and we're sure we could never manage in a similar situation. I thought of our own times of tribulation with our oldest daughter who has frequented the cells of various prisons because of her drug addition. Each time I would realize she was entering the down side of the recovery/relapse cycle that has been her life, I would think, *I can't handle this again.* But of course, I always would. And always, in retrospect, I would wonder how.

God gave the answer that morning as I drove across the desert. The speaker on the tape said that while we have a generous God, He is not a wasteful God. He will supply all the grace we need, *when* we need it, and not before. It was one of those "ah ha" moments. The reason I don't understand how some people get through their circumstances is because God is not asking *me* to go through them. He is giving them the grace *they* need. I needn't live in fear of not being able to withstand should our daughter stumble and fall. If it happens, God will come in at exactly the right time with the exact measure of grace I need to not only endure, but to help her through it. What an awesome God we serve!

*When I consider thy heavens, the work of thy fingers,
the moon and stars, which thou hast ordained; what is
man that thou art mindful of him?*
Psalm 8:3-4

When my husband and I go to our favorite camping spot, I love sitting out by the campfire at night and looking at the stars. I swear there are more stars there than any place else in the world. My husband has a more scientific answer— something about being away from the city lights that dim the brilliance or some such nonsense. I'm still certain there are simply more in that particular place.

I can picture David sitting out at night in a place similar to this camping spot when He wrote the above Psalm. Contemplating the heavens, the vastness of it all, the number of stars and the fact that God knows the name of each (Psalm 147:4), the perfect organization all working in exact order, is an incredibly humbling experience.

What is man when compared to the majestic workings of God's universe? And yet He places us above all His creations and then, as David says in verse 5, *"Crowns us with glory and majesty."* We should fall to our knees in worshipful gratitude as we consider the truth of this Psalm. And we should consider it often. Unfortunately, that is seldom the case. Instead we go to Him each morning with our list of everything He must do to keep us happy that day. And that is just those of us who go to Him at all, and if the statistics are correct, that's only about 5% of the world's population.

So why did God place such an immense importance on man, making him just a little lower than Himself? My Bible tells me that He is all knowing, that He knew before the beginning of time who was going to do what (Romans 8:29). Yet, even knowing beforehand that the majority of men would condemn themselves to hell, He still made us in His image. I believe that even though there would be a comparative few who would come to Him, he wanted the companionship, the fellowship, and the relationship with those few. He wanted someone upon whom He could lavish His love, those who would gaze at His heavens and appreciate His awesome creation, a group of people, no matter how small, on whom He could generously bestow His blessings.

Man is completely undeserving of the place God gave him in His creation. As I said, we should live our lives in humble gratefulness for where He places us in His overall scheme of things.

Beware that thou forget not the Lord thy God when all
that thou hast multiplies...
Deuteronomy 8:11, 13

God was talking to the Israelites as they were about to enter the Promised Land. He knew the land was good (flowing with milk and honey). He knew they would have plenty to eat and nice houses to live in. Their wealth would greatly increase as would their flocks and herds. He also knew that with the good life would come the tendency to forget that it was He who brought them to it.

Several thousand years later, people are no different. When our circumstances are difficult: bad health, errant kids, financial hardships, broken relationships, etc., we run to God. We say we are searching for His presence, but what we are really seeking is His hand. We want Him to touch our situations, make them better, and make the pain go away. We want Him to pick us up and carry us into the Promised Land. In return, we make promises of our own. "If You will just make me well, I promise I'll start taking care of my health. If You will just straighten out that kid, I promise I will start spending more time with her. If You will just help me find a better paying job, I promise to practice good financial stewardship."

In His goodness, grace, and mercy, God will often bring relief from our adverse circumstances. However, I don't believe for one moment He does it because of our promises. He knows they will fall by the wayside as soon as the pain is alleviated.

One of my morning devotions was written by a young man who has aids. He was asking for prayer for himself and his parents who were having such a difficult time dealing with the reality of the situation. This brought thoughts of others that I know and love within my church and my own family who are currently facing difficult circumstances. I felt a great shame in my heart and a deep need to cry out to God for forgiveness.

My life is so good and so full and God has blessed me so abundantly. I should be using the gifts of my good health and my abundant free time (neither of which I deserve) to further His kingdom in whatever way I can. But what do I do? Yesterday I did nothing—took a nap, watched a movie, and felt sorry for myself. How much of God's precious gift of time I waste!

I don't want God to have to pull the rug out from under me, as He frequently did the Israelites, to keep me close to Him. My goal is a close intimate relationship with Him in the bad times and in the good times.

...but the Lord looketh on the heart.
1 Samuel 16-7

In various places throughout the Bible God says, *"Be ye holy, for I am holy."* And elsewhere in various ways, He tells us to be perfect. This has always confused me because I know that no matter how much work He does with me, I could never hope to attain any respectable degree of holiness—not in this lifetime, anyway. And perfection? Yeah, right. I sure see that in my future. And yet this is what He tells me and I know He is not going to tell me something that is impossible for me to do. Hence the confusion.

2 Corinthians 5:17 tells us, *"Therefore if any man be in Christ, he is a new creature; old things are passed away; behold all things are become new."* Then Romans 6:2 says that I am dead to sin. Another confusing concept and one that has occasionally caused me to doubt my salvation because there has certainly been sin in my life since becoming a Christian. However, as will usually happen when I dwell on something long enough, God brought it together for me in the above verse.

My confusion, and I don't believe I'm alone in my errant reasoning, came from thinking in terms of my flesh, my body, and my mind instead of my spirit and my heart. When Paul said I was dead to sin, he didn't mean I would never again sin. He simply meant I was dead to the effects of sin. Not to say I won't have to pay the consequences when I do something wrong, but sin can't touch my spirit if I recognize, confess, and turn from it.

Likewise, in the flesh, I can never be holy and perfect because of the sin that is still present. But as the above verse tells me, God looks at my heart, not my flesh in which there is no good thing (Romans 7:18).

Is my heart pure? I've given this some thought and I truly believe I can say yes. When I began considering the question, I had to be careful to separate my heart from my mind because I must admit, there are times when my thoughts are certainly less than pure. But my heart? Yes. From the very depths of it I want only to glorify and please God.

My prayer each morning is that every word I speak, every word I write, every thought I think, and every action I take that day will be to God's glory and please Him. And I know each night that I have fallen short of that goal, but I pray it again the next morning. Why would I continue to pray for something that I know in the natural I will never attain? Because that is the desire of my heart and I'm so very grateful that is what God sees when He looks at me.

...and lest I should be exalted above measure through the abundance of revelations, there was given to me a thorn in the flesh, the messenger of Satan to buffet me, lest I should be exalted above measure.
2 Corinthians 12:7

There's been much speculation concerning what Paul's "thorn in the flesh" was. The most popular theory is poor eyesight based on the fact that some of his letters to the churches were obviously dictated to someone else. But even the best guesses are just that—guesses, because God chose not to tell us. I believe He did that for a reason. If, for instance, we knew that his thorn in the flesh was poor eyesight, those of us who have the same infliction could relate to him. But the rest of us would just skim over these verses feeling they don't pertain to our lives.

Exactly what is a thorn in the flesh? It is imperfection within myself that I can neither eliminate nor correct. I believe everyone has at least one. It doesn't necessarily have to be a physical imperfection, though it certainly can be as none of us are physically perfect. It could be less than desirable traits, such as an out-of-control temper that we battle. Or it could even be something completely outside ourselves such as a close relative that consistently rubs us the wrong way but that we're pretty much stuck with for the rest of our lives.

I've just come to a realization recently of what my own personal thorn in the flesh is—the tendency to overeat compounded by a greater tendency to easily gain weight. I have cried out to God to please take away my appetite, or please change my metabolism, or even to make me happy with fat. All to no avail.

As I peddled away on my stationary bicycle one morning this week, I got an illuminating revelation from God. (I haven't yet figured out why He chooses my bicycle time to talk to me, but He does.) The revelation? Eating and weight are always going to be a challenge for me. After 30 years of battling it I should have caught on to that truth by now. But I suppose I was always hoping for something magical to happen and I would return to my teenage state of being able to eat anything without ever gaining an ounce.

Does this mean I will always have to be miserable and struggle? No. Like Paul, I accept it as a humbling fact that I cannot change and I depend on God's grace to help me to do what I need to do to minimize the problem. In 2 Corinthians 12:9, God tells me the reason I can have this peace, *"...my grace is sufficient for thee for my strength is made perfect in weakness."*

*In everything give thanks; for this is the will of God's
in Christ Jesus concerning you.*
1 Thessalonians 5:18

Why is it easy to give thanks at some times and so hard
at other times? Yesterday morning I woke tired, depressed,
and filled with guilt over my lack of commitment to my
"living program" (healthy eating, regular prayer and Bible
study, daily writing, exercise, etc). We are in the process of
moving from one house to another and I drug through the
day doing what needed to be done, but not doing it with joy
or commitment. I went to bed last night tired, in pain, and
discouraged.

Something happened this morning as I read my daily
devotions, which is the first thing I do each morning with
my coffee. It was an instant change, as though God unzipped
my head, took out all the negative thoughts, and replaced
them with optimism, hope, and joy. He filled my heart with
thanksgiving, gratitude, determination, and motivation.
What happened? What made the difference?

Moving is still a necessity. But now there is the excitement and the challenge of turning the house into a home (we
live in company housing so we have to work with what we
have). I still have to deal with the reality of how easy it is
for me to use anything as an excuse to toss aside my "living
program", but today I see the guilt as sure proof that God
hasn't given up on me. This tells me that, yes, I've fallen, but
it's time to get up, dust myself off, and jump back in. This is
a living program that God designed for me over many years
and 1 Thessalonians 5:24 tells me that, *"Faithful is he that
calleth you who will also do it."* So I know if I don't give up
and will just depend on Him and His help and guidance, I am
assured of victory.

Nothing about my circumstances changed from yesterday
morning to this morning. Yet the change in my attitude and

outlook has done a 180-degree turn. This is proof positive of the truth of Proverbs 23:7, *"...for as he thinketh in his heart, so is he."* God makes the difference. The change takes place on the inside, not on the outside.

I've always said that emotional, mental, and spiritual pain is a great motivator. I used to have a high pain threshold in these areas, but that's no longer the case. My desire for joy and peace took over this morning and the Holy Spirit opened my heart so that God could pour them in. Thank you, God.

If ye then, being evil, know how to give good gifts unto
your children, how much more shall your Father which
in heaven give good things to them that ask him?
Matthew 7:11

God's love for His children is perfect. We cannot comprehend a perfect love. I believe the closest we come to seeing it on this earth is the love of a mother for her child, but those of us who are parents know even that love falls woefully short of the love God has for us.

As busy parents, if a disciplining action is going to inconvenience us, we may tend to overlook a transgression from our child. Not God. The Bible tells us that whom He loves, He disciplines (Hebrews 12:6). Oh, it may seem we've gotten by with a wrong in the short term, but each and every one has its negative effect on us in some fashion. Even if it's only in the form of a guilty conscience (which I personally find to be the most painful form of chastisements). On the other hand, we parents may dish out a discipline that is much too harsh for the infraction committed by our child, simply because they caught us at the wrong time when we've had a bad day. Not God. His word tells us He is the same yesterday, today, and forever (Hebrews 13:8). His discipline is always fair and always consistent.

Just as God disciplines us because of His perfect love, He rewards us from that same love. It might appear that we get by without punishment for our sins, but it's only an illusion. Likewise, it may seem that our good goes unrewarded, but that too is an illusion. There may be nothing tangible to point to as a reward, but one of the greatest rewards is peace of mind and a feeling of well being. And He bestows these lavishly on those who are engaged in living the best they can for Him.

In the healthy parent/child relationship, punishments and rewards are not given for the benefit of the parent. They are for the betterment of the child. If exercised with love, fairness, and consistency, they teach the child right from wrong, proper boundaries, and help him to grow into a loving, compassionate, productive member of society who will, in turn, help to do the same for others.

That is what God's perfect love is attempting to accomplish with us. When He is urging me to pray, read my Bible, help others, tithe of my income, be patient, loving, and kind, it's not because He needs me to be that way for Him. No, He doesn't need anything, but He knows these are the things that ultimately bring me peace and joy, and as a Father with a perfect love for His child, this is His greatest desire for me.

Come now, and let us reason together, saith the Lord...
Isaiah 1:18

Reasoning. A timely topic. Our youngest daughter, the beautiful blonde, the sleek professional woman, the on-top-of-the-world yuppie called me just a few minutes ago, weeping uncontrollably. She tells me she has been drinking too much the last few weeks. She is suffering physically, mentally, emotionally, and spiritually. She hates herself. She is trying to analyze the situation, to reason her way through it.

Been there done that. My heart hurts for her. As soon as I hung up the phone I fell to my knees, crying out to God on her behalf. She's tormented because she hasn't mailed me promised pictures. She's neither written nor sent money to her sister as she has committed to doing. Little things? On the surface they may appear to be, but in reality they are representative of a much deeper truth, a life that is on a downward spiral, out of control.

Was she coming to me for advice and help, or simply for comfort? I don't know, but I think it was probably a little of both and I tried to supply a little of both. My main advice was to quit trying to analyze the why of the situation, quit looking for reasons. There are some things that defy reason and we simply have to accept them. Addiction and the propensity to addiction fall into this category. My husband has spent agonizing hours trying to figure out our oldest daughter's addictions and addictive behavior. It totally baffles him. I tell him he is spinning his wheels and wasting his time. There is no rhyme or reason to it.

And this precious youngest daughter needn't waste her time trying to reason through her dilemma. Her family has been wrought with addictions for generations. She must respect that and have a sincere godly fear of engaging in any activity that could be addictive for her. If knowing the safe, cutting-off point in drinking is a problem for her (which she says it is), then the wisest thing to do is simply not start. That was pretty much the essence of my advice to her. Except for the most important and most valuable piece, go to God with it and enlist His help. Anything she does on her own may have some temporary results, but positive permanent results can only come from Him.

...in the world ye shall have tribulation...
John 16:33

Enid Starkie, Irish literary critic, said, "Unhurt people are not much good in the world," and I believe this is absolutely true. I once had a boss who told me her life story while we were on a business trip. She truly had a fairy tale childhood with loving, nurturing parents and amiable siblings. She was not wealthy, but very well-to-do. She was married to the perfect man and they shared mutual adoration for each other. They both had bright careers. There simply had been no flaw in her life ever. And she was the most totally self-absorbed, self-centered, boring person I had ever met. Needless to say, she was at a loss for words when I told her *my* life story, which, I have to admit, I probably did more for the shock effect than out of a desire to share with her.

The truth is, God says there *will* be tribulations in this world. We cannot escape them so we must choose how we will deal with them. In the good times, we have to constantly and consistently work on strengthening our relationship with God and our spiritual maturity. That is our *only* assurance of being prepared for the times of sorrow and tribulations. If we have a strong faith and belief in God, we will have the courage to face any challenge, knowing that "this too shall pass." But we can't just go our merry way, living shallow surface lives and expect God to come through with the courage in our dark hour of need. We must have spiritual character-building habits that will store up that courage for us.

It's amazing to me the difference a strong relationship with God can make in the way we handle sorrow. My dad died years ago while I was still drinking heavily. I went to my mother's house and was absolutely no help or comfort ˈ ˀr. My brother and I got drunk on the way home from ˀral home the night before the funeral. I cried a lot, a whole lot. But in spite of my many tears, I never grieved. I didn't know how. I only knew how to drink and to cry.

My mother died just a few years ago when I had ten years of recovery and walking with God behind me. I spent the week before her death sitting in the hospital praying for her and the whole family and writing about my life with her. I cleaned her house and am still cleaning up messy situations she allowed in her life. I cried and still do occasionally, but they are healing tears. I believe my grieving process has progressed well and has been healthy. God gave me amazing strength, courage, and coping skills through that very trying time. Yes, we are going to have sorrows, but looking to God for our comfort and strength puts us on the side of angels.

*...and the disciples were called Christians first in
Antioch.*
Acts 11:26

Christianity is now 2000 years old. Exactly what is it? I
haven't a clue what the official dictionary definition is, but
I would say that in the simplest terms it means a follower
of Christ. But what does it mean to be a follower of Christ?
The first prerequisite would be belief that Christ is the Son of
God. He was born of a virgin who conceived miraculously
by the Holy Spirit. The true believer must also believe in the
crucifixion and that Jesus was resurrected from the dead after
three days. Though Christianity involves much more, this
is the basis, the foundation, and the facts which are neither
disputable nor debatable.

Whereas God gave many commands, rules, and regula-
tions to the believers before Christ, Jesus gave only one: that
we love one another as He loves us (John 13:34). I wonder
about that but, upon reflection, I realize that if we truly
followed that commandment there would be no need for any
others.

I often think of the price Jesus paid for us to have the
joy and assurance of our salvation. When He hung on the
cross, God laid the sins of every man that had ever existed
in the past and every one that will exist in the future on
Him. I know how I feel when I've done something I know I
shouldn't—very bad. How must He have felt with the sins
of billions of people laid to His charge? And then to have
God turn His back on Him because He had to go through it
so that we would have a plan of salvation. I cannot fathom
the agony.

Unfortunately, most Christians take God's incredible
gift for granted. We treat each other badly, toss out casual
prayers, and constantly focus on what we don't have instead
of the bountiful gifts we do have. This must make God very

sad and I wonder if sometimes He regrets the ultimate sacrifice of His most holy Son for a massive group of ingrates. I wouldn't be surprised, but then I am attributing human traits to Him and forgetting His perfect unconditional love (which I can't begin to comprehend).

God says in His word that I am His child, a joint heir with His Son, Jesus Christ (Romans 8:17). What a thought! My current goal is to bring that truth into my very inner being so that I may come to a real personal relationship with God, His Son, and the Holy Spirit.

My grace is sufficient for thee...
2 Corinthians 12:9

God's grace constantly amazes me. He is so very very generous with it and yet, He is efficient. He doesn't render it where it isn't needed or until it is needed. I remember when I had this illumination. Our oldest daughter was between prison terms (it's sad when a person measures time in that way), and about to enter the relapse phase of her seemingly endless cycle of addiction/recovery, addiction/recovery. I knew it was about to happen again. By that time, we were more than familiar with all the danger signals.

I was driving into town and my mind was in that dark place of dread. I was telling God I simply didn't think I could handle it again. That was when He brought the above verse to my mind. I looked to the past and realized that at the very time we had to face those situations, it had not seemed unbearable or even that difficult. We simply did what we had to do at the time—one step at a time. And each time God gave us the grace we needed to do what we needed to do when we needed to do it but not before.

The apprehension I was feeling at the moment of this insight was a result of me worrying about something that *might* happen in the future. God would give me the grace to handle it should it become a reality, but it was not a reality at the moment so there was no grace for it. Then it struck me, His grace is for what is happening, not what might happen. I honestly believe that at that moment my life suddenly became about 97% worry-free and has stayed that way. I now know I don't need to ever worry about what might happen because God's grace is going to cover everything that comes down the pike and there is nothing I can't handle with His help and grace. What a liberating experience that was for me. Just as a side note, we did have to face another relapse and another prison term with our daughter, but we all made it through fine by the grace of God. And it has proved to be one of the greatest blessings of her life and ours as we have watched what God has done with her and through her.

As I said in the beginning, God's grace is incredible and as this verse tells us, it is sufficient. Sufficient means that it is all we need. And it is but don't look for it before the need arises.

Stone #11

Wisdom

༄

For the LORD giveth wisdom: out of his mouth
cometh knowledge and understanding.
Proverbs 2:6

When wisdom entereth into thine heart...
Proverbs 2:10

It's not difficult these days to find a knowledgeable young person, especially in a society which puts great emphasis on education. After all, this is the information age and information screams at us from every direction. Logging on to the Internet gives instant access to a proliferation of facts. There is no excuse for ignorance on any subject of interest.

Unfortunately, too many people confuse knowledge with wisdom. The two have nothing to do with each other and are not interchangeable. Our college graduates emerge from the halls of education with their heads stuffed with facts (mostly useless), a degree in their hand, an optimistic twinkle in their eyes, thinking they are ready to take on the world. But all too often they can be found a year later disillusioned, and working in a field that has nothing to do with their education (if they are working at all).

I read once that a person with a college degree uses, over his lifetime, only 10% of what he learns obtaining that degree. Being a college graduate myself, I feel that percentage may be a little high. Don't think I'm knocking education. I absolutely believe in it. Though the knowledge acquired may be mostly useless information, the discipline, sense of self-esteem, and confidence that is gained is priceless. I do feel, however, that our education system falls far short in stressing the most important acquisition we can gain — wisdom.

In all fairness to our teachers and our schools, wisdom is never part of the curriculum for a very good reason: it can't be taught. It can, however, be learned. Acquiring it is what should be taught to our young people, starting in the sandboxes of kindergarten.

How would I go about teaching someone to learn something as ambiguous as wisdom? There is only one method of obtaining wisdom which is by experience. But the good news is that it doesn't have to be our own experiences that bring the wisdom. What needs to be stressed is that we don't have to bang our own head against the wall to know it hurts. We can save ourselves much pain by listening to the words of wisdom spoken by the person who *has* experienced the pain first-hand.

Solomon was the wisest man who ever lived. His book of Proverbs was written from first-hand experience. We would be wise to study his Proverbs and fashion our lives accordingly. It could save us a mountain of pain.

Pride goeth before destruction, and an haughty spirit
before a fall...
Proverbs 16:18

God hates pride. Psalm 101:5 tells us, "him that hath an high look and a proud heart will not I suffer." It is something I pray about constantly. I ask God to keep me humble so that He won't have to make me humble. I hate those humbling experiences.

If we ever have any doubt of God's views concerning pride, just take a quick trip through the Old Testament. Even those He called to do His work, His chosen ones: Moses, David, Solomon to mention a few, He had to take down a notch when they started to think too highly of themselves and made decisions without consulting Him. I don't want to be guilty of that. And yet, I often find myself in the middle of doing that very thing. An example:

My husband and I, though well past middle age (I don't know anyone who is 120-years-old so I can no longer pretend to be middle age), are blessed with extremely good health. A number of years ago I realized this was totally a gift from God because we lived an alcoholic lifestyle with all the accompanying bad health habits for several decades. When I had this revelation, I realized the gift of good health came with a responsibility, just as most of God's gifts do. I needed to do all I could to maintain that good health. So with much pushing and prodding from God, we have developed a healthy diet, an aggressive exercise program, a sensible vitamin regimen, and we get plenty of sleep, drink lots of water, and actively work to keep the stress out of our lives. Consequently, we have only been sick once (flu) in the last eleven years.

There is no doubt in my mind that this is a God-given miracle. Though the maintenance plan is ours to implement, even He supplies that guidance and motivation as I

Thessalonians 5:24 tells us, *"Faithful is He that calleth you, who will also do it."* But here is where the pride problem surfaces.

I have a tendency to judge and be critical of those who are sick all the time. My thoughts run like this, "Well, if you would just take care of yourself and do what I do, you wouldn't always have those problems." I want very much not to think that way. This is the pride that God hates. So I seek His forgiveness for my thoughts and ask Him to give me a compassionate heart towards those less fortunate than myself. Admittedly, my motives are not entirely pure, as this desire is brought about in part by fear. I don't want God to allow circumstance in my life that will make it possible for me to sympathize because of first-hand experience. However, often fear is a great motivator and if it will get me off my duff well, I believe God does allow it.

...but we have the mind of Christ.
1 Corinthians 2:16

This is an interesting verse, but what does it mean? It says I have the mind of Christ, and since I believe in a literal interpretation of the Bible, I believe I have the mind of Christ. Let's work through this concept and see where it takes us.

First of all, we must understand that Paul made this statement in his first letter to the Church of Corinth so we know he was speaking to Christians. There is no way the unbeliever can have the mind of Christ. As a matter-of-fact, verse 14 of the same chapter tells us, *"...the natural man (unbeliever) receiveth not the things of the Spirit of God: for they are foolishness unto him..."* Knowing some non-believers, I know this to be true. Most spiritual concepts: giving to get, helping others, total surrender as a road to freedom, etc., are completely foreign to non-believers. These ideas seem absurd, and all the arguing and examples in the world are not going to bring about a change of mind for them.

The Bible tells us that when we accept Jesus as our Savior, He comes to live within us, and it simply follows that He brings His mind with Him. So why isn't our thinking instantly changed at the moment of salvation? Why do we continue to harbor worldly, carnal thoughts? There are several reasons. God does not force us into anything and that includes a new way of thinking. He makes His blessings available to us, but it is our responsibility to receive them. It's a trade-off. In order to receive the blessings, we have to turn loose of the old to make room for the new. He will not allow our bad and His holiness to cohabitate. This fact also includes our thoughts.

It's true we possess a brand new nature at the moment of salvation, but the new nature has come to reside in a body that still houses the old nature. Allowing the new to take over is a process. As each old thought comes in, we must replace it with a Christ thought. It's just that simple, though not always easy. Our old way of thinking is deeply entrenched and is not going to disappear just because that is our desire.

The trick is to become very aware of our thinking. This in itself is quite a task since we're used to letting garbage wander in and out of our minds without any filtering, but it is possible. In the beginning, we may have to throw out thousands of thoughts a day. However, the process becomes easier as we persevere and time goes by. The fastest way to making the mind of Christ dominant in our life is to stay in His word and saturate ourselves with His thoughts and His ways.

The fear of the Lord is the beginning of wisdom...
Psalm 111:10

Noted financial advisor, Howard Ruff, said, "It wasn't raining when Noah built the ark." That speaks volumes about wisdom. It indicates, and rightly so, that wisdom is obeying God even if the circumstances indicate a different course. Our lives would be much simpler, easier, and more peaceful if we would just obey when He calls.

I haven't known too many wise people in my life. In some areas my dad was very wise. He accepted things pretty much as they were and he let very little upset him. His past must have haunted him on occasion, but apparently he had worked all that out with God because he never indicated that it visited him in the middle of the night. I would be inclined, on a moment's notice, to say my mother was wise, but giving it thought, I know that she wasn't. She was intelligent and had more than her share of common sense, but I shouldn't confuse these two qualities with wisdom because they aren't the same.

So what is wisdom? Going to my dictionary, this is what I find, "Knowledge of what is true or right coupled with just judgement, insight, sagacity." So what is true and right? Well, once again that is where the Bible comes in.

Solomon is said to have been the wisest man who ever lived. God gave him wisdom because when asked by God what he wanted from Him, Solomon, though he could have asked for riches and fame, asked for wisdom. So God gave him more wisdom than had ever before, and presumably ever since, been apportioned to any man. Incidentally, he also got the riches and fame he *didn't* ask for. At any rate, Solomon wrote most of the book of Proverbs, so I believe it is a very wise move to read them, study them, and incorporate them into our lives.

Wisdom is mostly attributed to old people and for good reason. Wisdom cannot be learned from books, nor can it be taught. Wisdom is only gained through experience and living. Does this mean all old people are wise? Unfortunately, no. Wisdom comes from drawing knowledge from our experiences and asking such questions as, "What can I learn from this?" "What did I do right or what did I do wrong?" and, "What could I have done differently that would have improved the outcome?" These are tough questions and most people don't want to ask them. Only the wise put themselves through the pain the questions bring.

Remember not the sins of my youth...
Psalm 25:7

I wish I could be young and have the knowledge I have now. I'm sure that makes me unique. Surely no other person has ever wished that. Of course, the very nature of the wish makes it an impossibility. The only way to get the wisdom I have now is through experience and experience can only come with time, and what does time do? It ages. So it is impossible to be young and know what I know now.

Many people my age just wish they could be young again, knowledge or no knowledge. Not me. I spent the majority of my life not having a clue and I sure don't want to go back to square one and start over. I'll stay where I am (as if I had a choice).

That is not to say there are no regrets in regards to my past for there are many. I look at pictures of my youth and it breaks my heart. I was very pretty and very intelligent, both true gifts from God. I took both for granted and used neither. I drank away 32-years (all of my youth) and was definitely not the mother I should have been. Regrets? Absolutely! Many of them. But I do not dwell on them because dwelling on regrets is one of the most unproductive uses of time in which a person can engage.

The youth today seem to be divided (not equally, unfortunately) into two groups. There are the movers and shakers who are super intelligent and are the future of our country. This group is somewhat scary to me because they don't think like I do (which may be because they are super intellegent). The other group the larger one is comprised of the kids who have their hair spiked, their skin tattooed, and every part of their body pierced. These kids scare me as much as the other group though for entirely different reasons. Whether we like it or not, they are also the future of our country. About the only intelligible word they say that can be repeated is, "Cool."

Perhaps time will change our youth. It always has. All we can do is hope the change will be a positive one.

But put ye on the Lord Jesus Christ, and make not
provision for the flesh to fulfil the lusts thereof.
Romans 13:14

Make no provision for the flesh in regard to its lusts.
Exactly what does this mean? When I went into recovery,
I was told to not allow my thoughts to linger on drinking.
The counselors told my husband to get all of the alcohol
out of the house before I got home (an impossibility since
he didn't know all of my hiding places). They warned me
against going into bars and continuing an association with
my former drinking buddies (difficult when it is your mate).
AA told me not to allow myself to get hungry, angry, lonely,
or tired because that was when I was at my most vulnerable
(a warning I must still follow after all these years). What
were all these people doing with their advice? Telling me to
make no provision for the flesh.

It is shear stupidity for a person to intentionally expose
himself to a situation that is a problem for him. I am convinced
that neither my husband nor I will ever again, with God's
continued help, take another drink. But we don't keep alcohol
in the house either. It's not because we are afraid, but simply
because it would serve no purpose and would not be wise. I
recently spent a week at my son and daughter-in-law's house
babysitting our grandson while they went to Florida. While
looking for a bowl one day, I opened the cabinet where they
kept the liquor. Seeing it certainly did not tempt me to take a
drink, but it did stir up all kinds of unpleasant memories and
feelings. Why put myself through that if it can be avoided?

Different people have different lusts that create flesh
problems. For instance, I feel that pornography is a vile
scheme from Satan. I find it disgusting and am not tempted
by it. For some, however, it has an irresistible lure and once
drawn to it, they can't seem to pull away. These people
certainly need to keep the pornographic books and pictures

out of their homes and stay away from the places and people that deal in such things.

We each know what our problem areas are, whether we want to admit it or not. I'm currently dealing with over-eating. I could tell myself that I'd bake a chocolate cake for my husband (who doesn't need it either) but that I won't eat any of it. Pure deception! Chocolate cake is definitely one of my weaknesses and I know myself well enough to know if it's here, I'll eat it. Therefore I avoid the cake mix aisle at the supermarket.

The first part of the above verse tells us how to keep from making provision for our flesh—put on the Lord Jesus Christ and in some areas it may have to be an ongoing process.

Stone #12

God's Peace

❧

And let the peace of God rule in your hearts...
Colossians 3:15

...to be spiritually minded is life and peace.
Romans 8:6

I happen to be one of those who believe every word of the Bible just as it is written. I believe it is the inspired word of God. And I believe in a literal interpretation. Therefore, having said all of that, it follows that I believe the above verse. And I do, it's just that I'm having a particularly difficult time experiencing the peace it refers to. According to this verse, there can only be one reason for the difficulty: my mind is obviously not set on the Spirit.

There are circumstances in my life right now that are not particularly to my liking (I know that will be shocking to some since most people don't have this problem). I'm frustrated because I don't have the solutions to change the circumstances. "Coincidentally" one of my morning devotions is about frustration (how *does* God do that?). The writer of the devotion defines frustration as "a deep chronic sense or state of insecurity and dissatisfaction arising from unresolved problems or unfulfilled needs." There could not be a more accurate description of how I am feeling. What does the writer suggest?

He takes us to Romans 8:20-21, *"For the creature was made subject to vanity, not willingly, but by reason of him who had subjected the same in hope, because the creature itself also shall be delivered from the bondage of corruption into the glorious liberty of the children of God."* It appears that God Himself allows my frustration. Why? Well, this verse tells me that it is for the purpose of liberating me from bondage to take me into a glorious freedom. Boy! I sure want that. He goes on to say that when I am in the middle of frustration I should remember that God is in the process of revealing a great lesson to me and that He allows the frustration to build so I will be driven to Him in prayer.

He ends the devotion by telling me if I'm feeling frustrated I should rejoice because that means God is at work in my life. I understand the concept here and I totally agree. However, I'm having a little difficulty with the rejoice part. But I know that it works. Why do we balk at doing those things that we know will work for us and bring us out of an unpleasant state, whether it be frustration, anger, depression, or just plain ugliness?

Actually, the answer here is pretty simple. I have a choice. I can choose to stay in my frustration, fuming and stewing around for answers, or I can choose to take my eyes off my circumstances and get them on God. Once I change my focus from the physical world to the spiritual realm, thank Him for the answers He is going to bring to me, and trust Him to be able to handle the situation, my life will get real sweet and peaceful. Having had enough practical experience in these matters to know that His way works *every* time, I believe I will once again make that choice. My goal is to reach the point of always making that choice instantly, *before* I spend days in turmoil.

For unto you is born this day in the city of David a
Saviour, which is Christ the Lord.
Luke 2:11

It's 5:30 a.m. Christmas morning. My husband and I are on our way to a little town about 300 miles from our home to visit our daughter who is in prison. Well, God *does* command us to take care of the poor and the widows and to visit those who are in prison.

This is a very unusual Christmas for us. No children home for the holidays. No big meal to fuss and worry over. Just the two of us. Contrary to my usual last minute, spend too much shopping frenzy of years gone by, I made a gift budget, adhered to it strictly, and was through by December 1. I even surprised our post mistress by getting all my Christmas cards and gifts in the mail early. Christmas dinner took about 40 minutes to put together yesterday evening. And, I might add, it was very good, with a traditional holiday flavor. Yes, it's definitely been a break from the usual.

Sometimes different is good. Not being caught up in all the "have tos" has given me time to reflect on the true meaning of Christmas. Don't get me wrong. I am worse than any little kid when it comes to the excitement of the season. I love the lights and the music, Santa Claus, family, snow, and the beautiful gifts. But this year I've been able to go beyond all that to the really important Gift. The One God gave all mankind in the form of His Son. What an incredible awesome love there was behind that Gift. How sad that we have reduced the love that originated this season to a little fat man in a red suit passing out gifts that won't be remembered in a week.

We received a coffee/espresso maker from our son and daughter-in-law for a Christmas gift. We don't drink espresso, and we just bought a new coffee pot last week, so I'm going to return it to the store and exchange it for something else.

I've agonized over this decision because I don't want to hurt our daughter-in-law's feelings because, of course, she was the one who bought it. The situation has caused me to pause and wonder about how little I agonize over decisions that must hurt God deeply. There is something terribly wrong in a world where we worry more about hurt feelings concerning a coffee pot than how God must feel over our rejection of *His* Gift.

It's a good Christmas for me. Future ones will hopefully bring back the joy of family around the tree. However, I pray that I will always remember what God has shown me this year: go ahead and enjoy all the tradition, but don't get caught up in the stress of spending too much money on the perfect gifts and too much time on the perfect meal. I want to keep the focus where it belongs on God's Gift to us.

Be still and know that I am God...
Psalm 46:10

This is one of those confusing verses for me. Be still and know that I am God? What does that mean?

We, as a society, don't like to be still. No, let me be a little more honest than that. We don't know *how* to be still. Or maybe I shouldn't speak for a whole society. So let me say *I* don't know how to be still.

After many, many, many years of being what I considered to be a praying Christian, what a shock it was for me to learn that prayer was supposed to be a two-way communication between me and God. I thought prayer meant getting my list together of what I needed God to do for me that particular day, running through the family—petitioning blessings where deserved and convictions where needed, asking forgiveness for my sins, and oh yes, thankfulness for my blessings (if I could think of any at the moment).

What a revelation that God wanted to talk to me! I mean, after all, what could He possibly have to say to me? I began to get occasional "messages" from Him during my prayer time. I'm not talking audible words, just impressions—short, concise, and clear. I slowly realized He had a lot to say to me. Sometimes it was just a feeling of His love for me. Often it was to reveal an area of my life that needed work. When these revelations started coming, I would argue, "No, not that, God! I'm not ready!" I soon learned it does no good to argue with Him. When He says it's time it's time. So, even though I was still doing most of the talking, He was able to slip in an insight or revelation during those times I would switch subjects or pause to take a breath. But it was infrequent.

I needed to learn to be still and know that He is God. I had spent years experimenting with meditation (once even paying for instruction). I was never good at it. My mind simply wouldn't quieten enough for me to get into any kind of meditative state (a fact for which I am now most grateful). Somehow I related my failure at meditation to being unable to be still. Slowly I learned the two were in no way related.

Going into the presence of God and being still before Him does not mean emptying my mind and chanting a mantra over and over. Being still means to realize the awesomeness of God and to quieten my mind so that I can focus on His holiness. When I bask in the brightness of His light, forgetting my own selfish desires, He is able to talk to me completing the conversation cycle.

*And the peace of God which passeth all understanding
shall keep your hearts and minds through Christ Jesus.*
Philippians 4:7

I read from several devotional books in the mornings
during my quiet time with God. One of them is a prayer
companion that is published and sent quarterly. I have about
four year's worth and decided to recycle this year rather than
continue to purchase them. Each day of the book consists
of a verse, a short devotional pertaining to the verse, and a
page to write prayer requests and thoughts of thanksgiving.
It's been an interesting experience, reading my concerns of
four years ago.

It just so happens that the first book I picked to recycle
covered the period our oldest daughter was last released
from prison (coincidence? yeah right). My fears nearly leap
off the pages. Day after day I was actually begging God to
keep her close, remind her of all she's learned, don't let her
stray, etc.

She is now approaching another release from prison.
This time, however, there is no lump in my stomach, no
anxiety gripping my heart, no frantic fear racing through my
thoughts. There is only the calm peaceful knowledge that
God is in control. What is the difference between this time
and four years ago? Is it her? Is it me?

I believe the real answer to this question is that it is
both of us, but only through God. There has been no myste-
rious "event" that happened suddenly, changing my life and
opening my eyes. No, it has been more of a progressive
journey towards the truth of God's love and the reality of
His plan for our lives. I have finally opened up and allowed
God access to my innermost being where true change must
begin.

This beautiful daughter has come to know God in a
powerful way. He is real to her. She has faced the ugliness in

her life. She has laid it at His feet and accepted His forgive-ness. She no longer says or does the things that she thinks will please others. She wants only to please Him and realizes that will often include decisions that will not be popular with others. She is now willing to take that risk.

I have learned that any idea of control that I may think I have over others is only an illusion. I have learned to give the mistakes I made raising her to God and trust Him to keep His promise to work all things together for the good (Romans 8:28). And I know He will. The combination of all these gifts from God make it possible for me to face this prison release with gratefulness, excitement, and anticipation instead of the dread, worry, and anxiety of the past.

Rejoice in the Lord always: and again I say, Rejoice.
Let your moderation be known unto all men. The Lord
is at hand. Be careful for nothing; but in every thing
by prayer and supplication with thanksgiving let your
requests be made known to God. And the peace of
God, which passeth all understanding, shall keep your
hearts and minds through Christ Jesus.
Philippians 4:4-7

This was my first verse to memorize when I began my verse memorization program. I wanted to start with verse 5, *"Be anxious for nothing* "because that's the part that interested me. But I felt God telling me verse 4, *"rejoicing always"* was an integral part of being anxious for nothing.

So much of my life had been spent in worry and anxiety and I finally reached that place where I wanted more than anything this... *"peace of God which passeth all understanding."* I knew that my worry and anxiety were self-induced, but I didn't know how to stop it. I thought it was totally a mind thing. After all, Proverbs 23:7 tells us that, "As a man thinks, so he is." Or at least that's the way I always quoted the verse. What it actually says is, *"...as he thinketh in his heart, so is he...."* There is a difference between just letting thoughts wander in and out and actually *thinking in our heart*. Let me explain.

I can tell my subconscious just about anything. But if my actions are not consistent with my words, my subconscious is not going to buy what I'm saying. That was where the breakdown was with me. I knew all the right things to think, all the right words to say. After all, I had listened to thousands of hours of tapes, read all the success books, and knew by heart all the positive affirmations. So why wasn't it working? If I was doing everything right, why was I still worried and anxious all the time? Actually, the more I learned, the more anxious I became.

Suddenly one day the light dawned. Knowing all the right stuff, saying all the right words, and thinking all the right thoughts were not worth a hill of beans if I did not do what I had learned. Our oldest daughter once said to me, "Remember Mom, how when we were growing up, you always told us we could be anything we wanted to be?" I acknowledged that I did remember saying that frequently. She then said, "Well, you forgot to tell us we had to work for it." I laughed at the time, but I now know what she meant.

God does not intend for us to live an anxiety-filled life. He wants to give us His peace—the peace that passeth all understanding. I can't say I totally live in that peace, but I've seen enough of it to know I want more. The solution is to take everything to God, leave it with Him, and be willing to be whatever part of the answer He requires. Not always easy, but always simple, and always possible.

Therefore, being justified by faith, we have peace with
God through our Lord Jesus Christ.
Romans 5:1

Justified means (speaking of sin), "just as though it never happened." As the above verse says, this happens by faith. If we think about it, this only makes sense. Nothing in the physical world can "blot" out our sins.

I'm still dealing with the guilt in my life and searching God's Word for my answers. This is one of the verses I have discovered in my quest. If I am justified, and as a born again believer I have God's promise that I am, why am I not experiencing the peace that is promised in this verse? Obviously the problem is with me because I'm told very plainly that it is available to me.

I don't believe my past sins, and they were many, are the reason for the guilt I experience in my life today. I say "don't think" because I'm not absolutely certain. I know there is no individual wrong or wrongs that haunt me, but there may be an overall pervasive feeling of unworthiness left from the past. I'm just not certain what part that plays in this.

As I've said before, my problem seems to be in the little everyday things I don't do but think I should, or that I do but think I shouldn't. If I get up in the morning, am pleasant to my husband, do my exercises, pray, repeat my memory verses, do my writing, accomplish work-related duties, walk my dog, watch carefully what I eat, work on my book, cook a good dinner, and spend time watching TV with my husband well, then I feel relatively good about myself when I go to bed. But let me leave out just one of those things and that's what I focus on. And often, if I can't do all of them, I just won't do any of them.

I know I am a perfectionist. That is a major problem — if I can't do it perfectly, I won't do it at all. I'm too hard on myself. Jesus may forgive me, but I can't forgive myself.

Another problem, and I'm beginning to see it as a major factor here, is I still haven't attained that much sought after balance in my life. I still harbor that "all or nothing" mentality. "So what if I don't have the hour to work on my book today that I have vowed to spend. Use the 30-minutes I *do* have." Sadly, this has not been my mode of thinking. Instead, it's more like, "Don't have a full hour? Don't do it at all."

I don't have the peace of God promised in the above verse because I haven't allowed myself to receive it. It's out there with my name on it. I thank you, my readers, for allowing me to use this book as a vehicle to work my way to it.

Printed in the United States
200381BV00002B/298-333/A